⚞ Praise for *Look* ⚟

"Jim Gilmore teaches us that something as seemingly simple as looking can be crucial for success in any field. So get this book—and learn to look with whole new eyes."

—**DANIEL H. PINK,** Author of *Drive* and *A Whole New Mind*

"This book should be required reading in every design class and by every design team."

—**MARK GREINER,** Senior Vice President, Business Concept Design &
Chief Experience Officer at Steelcase Inc.

"Gilmore's Six Looking Glasses provide a powerfully simple tool for helping travelers to see the world more richly. Pack them in your suitcase and enjoy the view with fresh eyes!"

—**CHIP CONLEY,** Head of Global Hospitality & Strategy at Airbnb

"After reading Jim Gilmore's new book, you will never look at the world—including healthcare—in the same way again."

—**ROLF BENIRSCHKE,** Chief Patient Officer of Legacy Health Strategies

"Gilmore's *The Experience Economy* brilliantly anticipated a new economy based not on goods and services but on memorable experiences. This time around, he brings his unique perspective to the much-ignored power of observational skills. Take a good look at *Look*."

—**LEE KNIGHT,** Founder & CEO of Exhibitor Media Group

"Once again, Jim Gilmore challenges organizations to find unique ways to drive innovation. The power of observation has long been extolled but rarely emphasized in business. Jim's latest work will make all of us view our businesses through different lenses—and literally open our eyes."

—**DAVID PECKINPAUGH,** President of Maritz Global Events

"Our culture is increasingly distracted. With eyes glued to screens, we are often oblivious to the people beside us and the places we inhabit. The ancient rebuke of God could certainly apply to our generation, 'You have eyes but you do not see.' Our failure to recognize the world around us is especially dangerous for those seeking innovative ideas because, as Gilmore reminds us, what we see determines what we think and do. Seeing differently is one of Gilmore's specialties. He is one of the most gifted observers I know. Five minutes with him will convince you that ordinary objects and processes are overflowing with untapped potential—from airline seats to food preparation—if we could just learn to see them with new eyes. In *Look* he shares his simple but profound observational methods using Six Looking Glasses. Once you see the world with this tool, you won't see it, or your work, the same way again."

—**SKYE JETHANI,** Author of *With* and *Futureville* and Co-host of *The Phil Vischer Podcast*

LOOK

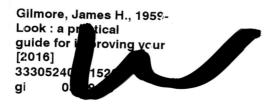

LOOK

A Practical Guide for
Improving Your Observational Skills

JAMES H. GILMORE

GREENLEAF
BOOK GROUP PRESS

Published by Greenleaf Book Group Press
Austin, Texas
www.gbgpress.com

Copyright ©2016 Strategic Horizons LLP

All rights reserved.

Distributed by Greenleaf Book Group

For ordering information or special discounts for bulk purchases, please contact Greenleaf Book Group at PO Box 91869, Austin, TX 78709, 512.891.6100.

Design and composition by Greenleaf Book Group
Cover design by Greenleaf Book Group
Looking Glass icons by Dave Szalay Design + Illustration, ©Strategic Horizons LLP.

Cataloging-in-Publication data is available.

Print ISBN: 978-1-62634-299-6

eBook ISBN: 978-1-62634-300-9

Part of the Tree Neutral® program, which offsets the number of trees consumed in the production and printing of this book by taking proactive steps, such as planting trees in direct proportion to the number of trees used: www.treeneutral.com

Printed in the United States of America on acid-free paper

16 17 18 19 20 21   10 9 8 7 6 5 4 3 2 1

First Edition

TreeNeutral

To Dr. Edward de Bono

CONTENTS

INTRODUCTION

In the summer of 2012, I delivered a keynote presentation in Atlanta at the annual conference of the Creative Problem Solving Institute (CPSI). The day before the talk, I attended a preconference workshop conducted by Mary Ellyn Vicksta and Natalie Jenkins, both certified experts in the lateral thinking methodologies of Dr. Edward de Bono (a credential I shared in an earlier stage of my career). The two women promised to introduce a framework that integrated the methods of Dr. de Bono with formal brainstorming as championed by Alex Osborn and his CPSI followers. I was not going to miss this session for there has long been some friction between the de Bono and Osborn camps. For starters, in chapter 15 of his groundbreaking book, *Lateral Thinking: Creativity Step by Step*, de Bono characterizes brainstorming as a "relatively minor setting" for creativity, not to be equated with any thinking process per se. (Ouch!) So I wanted to see how these two facilitators were going to accomplish this feat.

The Six Looking Glasses method was conceived during that workshop. Early in the session, participants were asked to collectively identify all of the de Bono techniques with which they were familiar. As my tablemates named various tools, inevitably the Six Thinking Hats method was mentioned. I then added, "Don't forget Six Action Shoes." I was met with blank stares, and understandably so, for the Six Action Shoes method never gained the same level of familiarity as de Bono's Six Thinking Hats. I explained that just as Six Thinking Hats outlined six different thinking modes, Six Action Shoes described six distinct action styles. After a brief discussion of this footwear framework, our table returned to identifying yet more de Bono tools, followed by other exercises introduced by our workshop leaders. But I quietly withdrew from the group, buried my head in my notebook, and started feverishly scrawling notes to flesh out my realization: the opportunity to create Six Looking Glasses!

Just as Six Action Shoes provided a useful tool for taking action within organizations, and Six Thinking Hats helped foster more robust thinking among individuals and groups, there was a need for a similar tool to help people more richly observe the world around them. Indeed, observation is the fountainhead from which any and all subsequent thought and action takes place. We don't think and act in a vacuum. When it comes to creating value in the world, this simple progression is always at work:

Looking ⟶ *Thinking* ⟶ *Acting*

Simply put: What you look at informs what you think about, which influences what you act upon.

More broadly: Observations about the everyday world lead to thoughts about possible ways to adjust, modify, reshape, reform, transform, or even overthrow aspects of that world, which when acted upon can actually help improve the world.

Recognizing this flow is critically important. Why? Because acting without thinking runs the risk of taking foolish actions, and thinking without first looking runs the risk of generating frivolous thoughts.

Consider this same progression from a right-to-left perspective:

Looking ⟵ *Thinking* ⟵ *Acting*

Creating any value requires taking certain action. But this begs the question: What thoughts are worth acting upon? And this in turn begs the question: What observations are best thought about?

It all starts with looking.

Before delving any further, now would be a good time to outline the basic flow of de Bono's approach to lateral thinking. There is certainly much more to lateral thinking than what will be outlined here, but these four steps provide a way of understanding the basic spine of de Bono's teachings about creativity. The four steps are

1. focus,

2. provocation,

3. movement, and

4. harvesting.

Each of these steps involves thinking as a skill, and as such can be improved upon with practice:

- *Focus* involves identifying what one wants ideas about.

- *Provocation* requires setting up mental stimuli for intentionally thinking differently about any chosen focus; it issues a provocative challenge to the current paradigm.

- *Movement* responds to provocations and challenges by deliberately moving past the same old familiar ideas and moving instead to truly new thoughts.

- *Harvesting* seeks to capture the value of the creative output by recognizing newness of thought regardless of its initial level of specificity.

Again, each of the above steps represents a learnable skill. We'll not address each step here. For that, read de Bono's book, *Serious Creativity*. Better yet, view some videos of Dr. de Bono posted online. Or best of all, find an occasion to watch him lecture live.

For our purposes, let's just focus on focusing. Why? Because focusing seems so very akin to looking, and I wish to make a distinction. Looking precedes thinking. Looking is pre-thinking, and therefore it's pre-focus. Looking is opening up to myriad aspects of the world that one might choose to focus upon for thinking (versus holding to the assumptions in your mind about a world unobserved). Looking establishes the context for focusing. It helps bring the world into focus.

Focusing without first looking runs the risk of limiting the output of thinking, and reducing the possible set of resulting actions that might eventually be considered.

The first rule of creativity: The easiest way to get a new idea is to think about something no one has ever thought about before.

The second rule of creativity: The easiest way to think about something no one has thought about before is to look at something in a way no one has ever looked before.

This book presents a practical method for improving anyone's observational skills. For every day we have opportunities to look in new and different ways. We all can and will notice more, so much more—if we just learn to look.

LEARNING
TO
LOOK

1

WHY LOOK?

W e spend most all of our lives with our eyes open. Yet there are different degrees to which we use our open eyes. The very phrase "eyes wide open" suggests there are many occasions when our open eyes are not completely open, when we miss perceiving some aspect of the world before us. Indeed, we are often inattentive to what exists right around us.

We look, but we don't see. And we don't see, because we're not really there, looking. This "being elsewhere" is particularly pronounced in an age of distraction, exemplified by the pedtextrian (a term someone coined for a pedestrian texting while walking), or the screenager, which includes any of us using digital devices while not walking. I have witnessed many screenagers (usually at an airport) three screens deep, with laptop, tablet, and smartphone—all turned on, commanding complete and divided attention. There is not much looking going on in such circumstances—at least not at the embodied world in which one is immediately situated. Interestingly, observing this three-screens-deep behavior triggered this thought: Screens were once things we only looked at, but then we started holding screens; then we started touching them. Now, people are starting to wear screens on their wrists, arms, heads, and even torsos. Are digital implants next?

To really look is to make an observation such as this noticeable progression. To look takes note of something as important or meaningful. It is the kind of observation that registers an "aha." It is the kind of looking that sees something anew. It is a way of noticing.

Such noticing is not easy. The inability to see something can strike us even when we are most consciously and intently looking. Most of us have had the experience of looking for some misplaced item, growing ever more frustrated by our inability to locate it, and only after we have "looked everywhere" (or so we say) does the lost item suddenly appear.

Let me share a true story of one such incident. It was the evening of my wedding. After the ceremony and reception, close friends and family gathered at my in-laws' home to spend some additional time together. At the end of the night, all the men who had worn rented tuxedos collected their garments—shoes, pants, jackets, shirts, ties, and so forth—and put them in a pile to be returned en masse the next day. As we made an accounting of all the items, one piece was missing: one last cummerbund. Everyone frantically searched the house for the wayward cummerbund. After what seemed like an eternity, we gave up the hunt, resigned to pay whatever penalty would be incurred the next day. It was then that someone noticed the cummerbund. My father was still wearing it! The cummerbund had been curled up around my dad's waist the whole time, unnoticed, under his belly.

Why look? We need to look in order to notice that which we do not normally see. We must come to recognize the value to be had in making new discoveries of people and places, products and processes, and objects and occasions that otherwise sit unnoticed, along the underbelly of everyday life.

But seriously: Why look?

First of all, take a step back and consider that the world is intrinsically worth looking at. Both nature (nurtured by mankind) and artificial environments (constructed by mankind) are wondrously created. To not see this is to not be human. We should look in order to better appreciate the circumstances in which we are situated in our work, our homes, our communities, our schools, our churches, and our recreations.

Secondly, there is so much variation in the world to be compared. In making comparisons—within any field of study—greater understanding is gained. Without looking for this kind of comparative understanding, all thought and action stagnates. We should look in order to change the context in which certain problems and issues are understood and addressed.

Thirdly, what matters does not just exist in a single field of study. There are worlds and worlds of details existing in many different disciplines. Just as value can be unlocked by making comparisons within an individual field, opportunities for new insights often only emerge when looking across multiple disciplines. Such cross-disciplinary looking is too often neglected in the present era of specialization. Some breakthroughs may only come when specialists look more richly outside their normal purview. We should look in order to alter the state of mind with which we approach any situation.

Fourthly, a surface-level understanding of the world and a superficial approach to problem-solving will not suffice to address many critical problems faced today locally, regionally, nationally, and globally. Opportunities to better address these concerns will only emerge when life is examined up close and in detail. We should look in order to be more attentive to what really matters.

Fifthly, the world can be made a better place. Beyond the world's known problems, other real troubles often exist unseen or ignored in society. These troubles need to be brought to light. And our known problems are often addressed via the same tired old paradigms. We should look in order to release new energies into the marketplace of ideas and action.

Finally, take a look back at the reasons cited. Does anything seem missing? Has something gone unnoticed in sharing this list? Surely it's this: Looking itself has intrinsic worth. Looking is pleasurable. A life spent looking is a life worth living. And those who routinely and richly look are generally much more interesting and more influential people than those who don't! We should look just to be dutifully present in the world.

It should be clear: We need to invest more time looking. We need to take the time to learn to more skillfully look in order to help make us better observers, and thus more creative thinkers and more innovative practitioners in the various callings in which we labor. Take heart: The Six Looking Glasses method promises to guide you to become a more skilled observer by enriching your time spent looking.

We will introduce the Six Looking Glasses tool a few chapters from now. Before doing that, however, let's briefly examine looking as a skill and the role of wearing glasses to improve sight.

2

LOOKING AS A SKILL

Want to be more skilled at observing? One word of advice: Look. Not satisfied with that one-word exhortation? Here are two: Pay attention. These two words capture the very essence of looking as a skill. To learn to look, you need to learn to pay attention.

Many of us, too many of us, take our sight for granted. Sure, we look. But we pay little attention to our looking. We seldom stop in our tracks to just look and listen to what is there to see and hear. We're often so busy, so on the go, that we're too distracted to really look.

So stop, look, and listen. Paying attention is just that.

Interestingly, these three words comprise the title of my favorite childhood book—*Stop Look Listen* by Virginia Mathews—that I recall reading over and over as a little boy. These three verbs define what it means to pay attention.

Now let me ask you this: What do you recall as your favorite childhood book?

I have asked that question to countless people, and based on their responses—which include many aha moments of self-discovery for those answering—have concluded that identifying your favorite childhood book reveals much about your calling, or who you are. (Perhaps you are having such an aha moment right now!) There is a reason that particular book resonated with you as a child.

Listen to what Os Guinness has to say in his book, *The Call: Finding and Fulfilling the Central Purpose of Your Life*. Guinness writes, "Calling reverses the way most people think. . . . Instead of 'You are what you do,' calling says, 'Do what you are.'"

Want to improve how skillfully you look? Start with taking a good look at who you are. Look at yourself. That may and should strike you as odd advice for the topic of how to develop the skill of looking. But paying attention to who you are will help you pay more attention to where you are. Why? Because how you see yourself influences what you see when you look.

David Finn, an acclaimed professional photographer and lifelong New Yorker, wrote a fascinating book, *How to Look at Everything*. (How do you not take hold of this book when you see that title on the shelf?) Finn recounts how he was affected by a single photograph he took while amassing a portfolio of shots for use in a book documenting life in New York City. This particular photo was taken out a car window and captured a man walking down the street while reading a book (a pedtextrian in the predigital age). Only after Finn had developed the film, did he notice a second man seated on a stoop as the reader-walker went by. The juxtaposition of the two men made for a most arresting image, one that prompted inner refection. Finn shares his epiphany, "Why did I consider it such a revelation? Why did so many familiar sights now look so different? It was because I had never looked so intently at the scenes of daily life before. And as I looked through my viewfinder, my mind gave new meaning to what I was seeing. I saw more than what was there because I was paying such close attention to what I was photographing." Finn no longer saw himself as just a photographer, but rather a "walker in the city." This different look at himself transformed his ability to look outside himself.

Want to be more skilled at looking? Look at yourself. Look intently at the scenes of your daily life. Pay closer attention to where you are and what you are doing. See yourself as an observer, a walker in your city.

Stop. Look. Listen.

⚡ 3 ⚡

WEARING GLASSES

In fourth grade a major event happened in my life. The results of a routine physical examination at school concluded that I should visit an optometrist. Further tests confirmed that I needed eyeglasses. Devastated by the news, I remember crying. (I suspect many children receive this news the same way.) But good news soon followed. Having previously been a B/C student, my grades suddenly improved. I started to get straight As. No one—not my parents, not my teachers, not myself—had previously realized that my eyesight was deficient. I had been "wearing" bad eyesight like a hidden cummerbund. But by wearing glasses, I could see like never before—and my grades proved it.

Looking is a skill that can often be aided with better viewfinders—to borrow the term used by David Finn to describe the lens through which he sees the world. Better viewfinders—looking glasses—are employed in any number of situations to improve looking. A hunter may use a scope to lock in on his prey. A soldier might wear night goggles to see in the dark. A submarine commander must rely upon a periscope to look above the surface of the water. A jeweler may use a monocular to examine the quality and cut of a diamond. A physician uses a gastroscope to peer inside a patient's stomach. An astronomer employs a telescope to see the stars. And most all of us use sunglasses to cut the sun's glare.

Wearing these glasses helps us see the world in ways that we cannot without them. So it is with "wearing" the Six Looking Glasses—using each in different circumstances, based on the particular observational needs of the moment.

This then is the twofold premise for wearing any of the Six Looking Glasses:

- Looking is a skill; more precisely, looking is a set of skills.

- That set of skills can be greatly enhanced through the use of a distinct set of looking glasses.

☀ 4 ☀

THE SIX LOOKING GLASSES

Each of the Six Looking Glasses promotes a different way of making observations. Each functions uniquely as a particular kind of viewfinder. To assist with remembering these six looking functions, each method of looking is metaphorically associated with a particular device or apparatus used to enhance one's looking, to help see and discover.

Each function should be readily understood based upon the name of the associated device and its primary purpose. For example:

- **Binoculars** are used to look across and survey at a distance.

- **Bifocals** are used to alternatingly look between two contrasting views or directions.

- **Magnifying glasses** are used to look closely at one main spot.

- **Microscopes** are used to look around for more and greater details.

- **Rose-colored glasses** are used to look at something better than it actually is.

- **Blindfolds** are used to look back and recall.

Assigning each function to a particular way of looking yields the Six Looking Glasses, or six ways of looking.

🔭 BINOCULARS LOOKING

Binoculars are useful when you "can't see the forest for the trees." Binoculars looking takes place at a distance from what is being observed, surveying and scanning for what might be noteworthy. This type of looking determines what may be worth examining with other looking glasses. Binoculars looking involves taking a step or two back from the situation and picking a vantage point to better observe the overall scene.

∖ᴏ̀ BIFOCALS LOOKING

Bifocals looking takes two alternating views of any given situation or circumstance. Looking with bifocals compares and contrasts different aspects of what's being observed, seeking to uncover various levels and layers of significance. This type of looking either pairs obvious opposites, or it looks for not-so-obvious combinations to pair as opposites. Bifocals looking then alternates between these two different or opposing views.

ᛘ MAGNIFYING–GLASS LOOKING

A magnifying glass spots one thing to look at more closely. Magnifying-glass looking takes a break from other ways of looking to examine one particular feature in more detail. It pinpoints that which may not otherwise be seen as significant, taking time to put everything else aside in order to look "up close and personal." Magnifying-glass looking spots something to be seen inside the overall scene.

⚗ MICROSCOPE LOOKING

Looking with a microscope involves looking for more and greater details. Rather than zeroing in on one particular point, microscope looking slides up and down, left and right, seeking to identify yet more features worth examining. It looks around. It often explores the scene by shifting the viewed object itself—to observe even more details at the edges of the scene. Microscope looking involves scrutinizing and studying the scene.

ᴏ⊸ ROSE–COLORED–GLASSES LOOKING

Looking with rose-colored glasses sees the potential that may not be readily apparent when using the other looking glasses. This view looks past readily apparent flaws to observe the opportunities that could be and maybe should be there. Rose-colored glasses look ahead to improve the scene by uncovering hidden opportunities.

🐾 BLINDFOLD LOOKING

Blindfold looking is "looking at looking." In this regard, it fundamentally differs from the other five looking glasses. This may seem counterintuitive—and it is! But therein resides its usefulness. Having employed the other ways of looking, blindfold looking reflects upon and recalls what was seen (or not seen) and how it was seen (or not). It serves to both summon what has already been noticed and to redirect further looking based on how and why something was missed or mistaken in the scene.

These different ways of looking should be referred to by their respective names: binoculars looking, bifocals looking, magnifying-glass looking, microscope looking, rose-colored-glasses looking, and blindfold looking. Once users of the Six Looking Glasses method become familiar with each way of looking, the individual function of each lens should quickly and easily come to mind. For example:

- "Let's get out our binoculars to survey."

- "We should all wear our bifocals now."

- "Try magnifying-glass looking and see what you spot."

- "Spend some time doing microscope looking for a while."

- "Don't be so upset at what you're seeing; put on your rose-colored glasses."

- "Okay now, let's switch to blindfold looking."

Theoretically, more types of glasses could be added to the portfolio: rifle-scope looking, night-goggles looking, periscope looking, monocular looking, gastroscope looking, telescope looking, or sunglasses looking, for example. But there is wisdom in picking just six. As Dr. de Bono likes to put it concerning Hats and Shoes: fewer than six is inadequate, more than six is cumbersome.

There are reasons certain types of glasses were excluded from the portfolio. A telescope can be considered supersized binoculars—for surveying at even greater distances. Night goggles and sunglasses are covered with bifocals looking, as night/day and bright/dark are particular kinds of opposites. And other glasses often have a too specialized use to be very useful as a metaphor.

The Six Looking Glasses offered here prove in practice to be a sufficient set of instruments for more richly looking at any situation.

Think of a set of golf clubs.[1] As the golfer proceeds to play a given hole, different types of clubs are used to make the way from tee-box to fairway to the green and then into the hole. First, the player takes out a driver. Then maybe a fairway wood or iron is used. Next comes a wedge. If necessary, a sand wedge might be called upon. Finally, the putter comes out of the bag. And somewhere along the line, a ball retriever may be summoned should a ball land in a water hazard. The basic process is to select a club, then use it.

The Six Looking Glasses method serves as a similar set of devices. An observer might begin with binoculars to survey the scene, and then don bifocals to look at something in two different ways. Next, the magnifying glass spots something of significance, followed by microscope looking to examine more details. Finally, rose-colored glasses see something better than it is. And somewhere along the line, blindfold looking is used to recall all that has been seen.

The process looks like this:

1. *Step 1: Select a looking glass.*

2. *Step 2: Observe using that particular way of looking.*

Then repeat Step 1 and Step 2. Choose each successive viewfinder in any order one chooses: there is no one right sequence for using the Six Looking Glasses. The looker is free to pick glasses in any order desired.

---

1   The golf club analogy is one de Bono has similarly used to illustrate the use of the Six Thinking Hats.

⚹ 5 ⚹

WHERE TO LOOK

L et the looking begin! But wait: At what are you going to direct your gaze? The process sounds simple enough: Select a looking glass and then use it. And it is. But the tool is also of no use to you (or anyone else) if you lack any notion of what to consciously and deliberately observe using the Six Looking Glasses.

So where should you look? Consider four choices: Nothing in particular, everything you encounter, anything at all, and something of interest. Let's go for a ride—yes, a ride!—and examine each option, one at a time.

LOOKING AT NOTHING IN PARTICULAR

To look at nothing will get you nowhere—if "nothing" means to be altogether indifferent to looking. But it can be useful to look at nothing in particular, if such looking means being open to anything that might become meaningful to you. This looking is not looking for some specific something; rather it is being constantly on guard, ever aware of the need to look, looking at everything you encounter.

LOOKING AT EVERYTHING YOU ENCOUNTER

To literally look at everything would be overwhelming. It would be unrealistic in any situation to take on the task of looking at every single thing, to the very last level of detail. You would never finish looking (let alone move on to thinking or acting). But it can be useful to look at everything you encounter, in terms of considering everything worthy of your gaze. This looking involves treating whatever unfolds in everyday life as a chance to look at anything you want, anything at all.

LOOKING AT ANYTHING AT ALL

You can of course look at anything you want—even if that thing is not anything you really care to observe. This might actually prove to be a fruitful practice. In fact, looking at something at random, anything at all, can often yield the most surprising benefits. Why? Because you may never have otherwise considered looking there! This type of looking means developing an interest in anything you want, as a matter of choice, so that you start looking at something of interest.

LOOKING AT SOMETHING OF INTEREST

To just glance at something is not really looking. To look with interest, to have an interest in something, involves a more meaningful kind of looking. It's to find something of interest beyond a surface-level understanding of the circumstances in which you find yourself or place yourself. Interestingly, this type of looking can take place even when you are looking at nothing in particular.

I trust you have noticed the Seuss-like circular logic in the descriptions presented above for these four areas of where to look. (If not, go back and look again.) Together they represent an attitude of looking, a habit of looking, and a discipline of looking. Where should you look? The simple answer is you should look somewhere, anywhere, everywhere, even in unusual "nowhere" places.

Many years ago, I took a transcontinental flight to Los Angeles. This was before 9/11, when I would pride myself on being the last to arrive at the gate, just before the airplane door would close. I had been upgraded to first class, and as I tucked my bag away in the overhead bin I noticed that my seating companion was going to be none other than the legendary comedian George Carlin.

Soon after I settled into my seat, Carlin grew fidgety. So I nonchalantly handed him an amusing article from *The Wall Street Journal* about "Pudding Man," a gentleman who had taken to purchasing all the pudding in grocery stores in the San Francisco Bay Area in order to collect and redeem the labels for twenty-five miles apiece in American Airlines' frequent flyer program. Carlin was enjoying the newspaper story when the flight attendant interrupted to ask about our meal preferences. I've never met anyone so precise in expressing his exact desires. Carlin requested the pasta dish— and asked that it be delivered at the last possible moment so it could be finished just before we would begin our final descent. In other words, he did not want the food delivered when the flight attendant wanted it delivered; rather, he wanted it later, so he would not be disturbed midflight.

Once airborne, Carlin took out his Mac notebook and typed nonstop. I took out my laptop as well, as I had a presentation to prepare for the next day. As we both worked away, I knew I must strike up a conversation at some point, and decided that I would do so when the pasta dish was delivered.

Hours later, as Carlin's meal was served, I turned to him and said, "Mr. Carlin . . ." "Yes," he responded coyly. "I just wanted to let you know how much I appreciate you not disturbing me during this flight." Carlin roared.

I had George Carlin laughing! I went on to confess that I had once come in second place in a high-school talent show as his Hippy Dippy Weatherman character. Carlin retorted, "Not bad, for being derivative."

I then shared my admiration of his observational skills and expressed my belief that most people were not very good at noticing the everyday world around them. Carlin took exception, at least in part, explaining that people in fact recognize the same things he notices—providing the basis for an appeal to a shared experience when making a joke. But he went on to explain that "the problem is that people just don't know where to put the data." He then shared that in his computer he maintained 2,500 different directories in which he recorded his everyday observations. And he knew his 2,500 categories.

I'm not suggesting you necessarily develop a list of 2,500 categories. But I will suggest a concrete method for choosing where to look that involves having twenty-four pre-determined categories for capturing your everyday observations.

LOOKING A TO XYZ

For each letter of the alphabet (and collapsing X, Y, and Z into a single bucket), identify one word beginning with that letter that you can associate with where you would like to look. Or, if you prefer, you can choose a word that identifies what you would like to look for or whom you would like to observe. Once you have your categories, commit them to memory as your ABCs of looking.

Here then is a simple workspace for recording your A to XYZ categories:

A	_____	M	_____
B	_____	N	_____
C	_____	O	_____
D	_____	P	_____
E	_____	Q	_____
F	_____	R	_____
G	_____	S	_____
H	_____	T	_____
I	_____	U	_____
J	_____	V	_____
K	_____	W	_____
L	_____	XYZ	_____

You can of course develop more than one A to XYZ list. Develop one hundred such lists (perhaps different lists for different domains of attention) and you'll have nearly as many categories as George Carlin!

6

LOOKING SHORT AND SLOW, LONG AND FAST

When we do most anything, we tend to operate in one of two ways. If we don't have much time, then it's short and fast. If we have plenty of time, then more likely we go long and slow. Hence the adage known as Parkinson's Law: Work expands so as to fill the time available for its completion.

Short-and-fast efforts focus on quick and easy tasks, ones we know we can readily do. In these cases, we want to "get 'er done," as comedian Larry Whitney, The Cable Guy, puts it.

On the other hand, long-and-slow efforts usually focus on more arduous tasks, ones we know will require sustained energy and a more paced approach. We're in it "for the long haul" in these instances.

Most of life's activities generally fall into one of these two modes of operation. As a result, it's our natural inclination to do one or the other. It is however a mistake to only employ either of these two tendencies when looking.

Taking one or both of these approaches may be precisely why so little fruitful looking takes place. Looking short and fast too easily overlooks things, because the looking is too rushed. The result is missed discoveries. Conversely, looking long and slow can bog things down. When any moment of looking is overly prolonged, we get too introspective and start thinking about ourselves instead of looking outside ourselves.

When looking, we need to learn two alternative approaches, ones in direct contrast to the normal ways of doing most activities. We need to embrace these two alternative modes of observation: (1) instead of short and fast, we need to look short and slow, and (2) instead of long and slow, we need to look long and fast.

LOOKING SHORT AND SLOW

If you don't have much time, look short and slow. Because time is short, the time is especially precious. Resist the temptation to rush the looking. Instead, take some time to first consider which of the Six Looking Glasses makes the most sense to use. Maybe time only allows for one looking glass. Which should it be? Or maybe there is only time for two looking glasses. Which combination makes the most sense to use? Make the most of the limited time available by selecting the few looking glasses that would be the most useful to don.

LOOKING LONG AND FAST

If conversely you have plenty of time, look long and fast. Resist the tendency to take extra time, prolonging the use of any one looking glass beyond what is necessary. Instead, take advantage of the abundance of time to rapidly use all Six Looking Glasses. By looking fast, you allow for the repeated use of some looking glasses. Go back and use different looking glasses a second and maybe third or more time. Make frequent transitions. Look iteratively. You're only wasting time when taking your time. When you do eventually have less time, you can then look short and slow!

Both of these counterintuitive approaches will result in better, richer looking. When you have little time, slow down and take your time; select just a few looking glasses to use and make the best use of them. When time is plentiful, pick up the pace; try to use all of the looking glasses multiple iterative times.

Of course, the use of the Six Looking Glasses with each of these approaches will greatly benefit from a more thorough understanding of the functionality of each one. It is to this task that we now turn.

BINOCULARS
LOOKING

≡ Scan the scene. Survey everything to see the options for further exploration.

≡ She is just looking it over to see what is there before probing any further.

≡ We're too close to the situation. Let's step back and look at this from a distance.

≡ Find a place to take in all the action from the best vantage point.

Some time ago, I was playing golf with three coworkers. It is useful to know in this tale that one player, Mark, prided himself in putting in significantly more hours at the office than the rest of us. Also note that we carried our own bags this day in lieu of driving carts. None of us were playing particularly well. On one hole, my drive landed off the right edge of the fairway, while Mark hit a shorter drive that went off to the left. After I arrived at my ball, I waited for Mark to hit, because he was farther to the green. But Mark was having difficulty finding his ball, so the other two players went to assist. Because I was clear on the other side of the fairway, I did not head across to join the effort. I figured the three of them would find Mark's ball soon enough on their own. I was so very wrong. Two minutes went by. Then another two. Then two more. Finally, tired of waiting, I trekked across the fairway and walked right up the lost ball.

As I pointed to his ball, I took a kindhearted jab at Mark and said, "It's not the quantity of time that you put in, it's the quality of time."

How had I managed to do this? Well, from across the other side of the fairway, looking at the three searching for Mark's ball, I paid attention to where they were wandering to and fro, and I soon noticed one particular patch of neglected turf. By keeping a distance, I had practiced binoculars looking. My vantage point provided a perspective that was unavailable to the others. Surveying from a distance had proved the key ingredient to success.

✷ 7 ✷

LOOKING ACROSS:
SURVEYING AND SCANNING

O ld war movies often depict generals mounted on horses or atop tanks. Or if they are on foot, they are often standing on high ground, overlooking the battle scene below. They avoid the front line not for any lack of bravery, but because their choice of position must allow for surveying the overall situation and recognizing the relationships between different flanks. They look across at a distance in order to best direct their troops. In such a position, binoculars greatly aid in performing this type of observation. In fact, binoculars are often essential to perform the task.

The essence of binoculars looking is scanning across the entire set of circumstances. Looking with binoculars concerns itself with seeing the "big picture." Its purpose is often to determine what other looking glasses should be used, and more importantly, to determine what areas and elements of the scene should be the target of subsequent looking.

While binoculars looking may tend to be performed by leaders, this type of looking can actually be done by any member of a group. For example, a frontline soldier might look up from the immediate battle, scan the opposing forces, notice unusual rear movements, and consequently alert the commanding officer of such developments. Binoculars looking is particularly helpful

- when entering a new place or situation,

- when circumstances change within a familiar place or situation, or

+ when time is limited and decisions have to be made quickly concerning where it's best to invest in more looking, thinking, and action.

For example, when entering an unfamiliar store for the very first time, you might want to use binoculars to familiarize yourself with the general layout of the place before shopping any particular aisle. Or if you're working a trade show booth and traffic suddenly drops, you might want to walk the floor and check the overall flow of the show. Are other booths also slow? Or just yours? This binoculars perspective might be useful before determining whether to adjust your actions to attract more guests to your booth, or if you should simply allocate more time to those few who do visit. Or suppose you are informed that your boss will not arrive in time to make a big presentation and you have just a few minutes to prepare to stand in. It would probably be more prudent to quickly scan through all the Power-Point slides to get the gist of the overall material rather than just reading the first few slides in full detail.

In each of these instances, the use of binoculars functions as a means to orient the looker. Surveying the overall scene and scanning for what elements may or may not be worth further examination make the observer more aware of all there is to consider. Binoculars looking also helps avoid jumping to conclusions by allowing the observer to take in the full picture.

Consider how often project teams, company strategists, executive decision-makers, product designers, and public policy makers would benefit from taking time to more frequently don binoculars. How often do completed projects fail to address certain key issues? How many times do companies miss opportunities that once-remote competitors instead see and exploit? Could many design flaws be avoided if designers stood back and considered the particular circumstances in which various goods, services, and experiences were to be consumed? (Ever buy something that looked good in the store but didn't work or fit when you got it back home? Chances are it looked good in the design studio as well, but during development the designers never stepped back and watched how actual users interacted with the product.) Aren't many of us frustrated by elected officials who fail to "get out of the policy weeds" to take a bigger—and more distant—look at the broader issues of the real world where laws and policies have to be implemented?

Binoculars looking scans across all objects in view. It surveys every option. It seeks to take in the overall context for looking, rather than focusing on specific details. As soon as you zoom in to make something the sole focus of your binoculars looking, it is generally time to switch to a different looking glass.

Binoculars are in fact seldom used alone. Generals, for example, after having identified something of interest via binoculars, often send scouts out to look up close at some matter in greater detail. They may hear reports coming back from these scouts and stop looking altogether in order to discuss, decide upon, or even postpone actions.

Often, periodic looks via binoculars are needed to see if anything has changed since the last time the scene was surveyed and scanned. Binoculars looking is often punctuated with such repeated use at various intervals.

Binoculars looking usually cannot by itself encompass all the looking that needs to be done in any given situation. But by taking a break from other forms of looking, the use of binoculars can often bring clarity to the looking (and to the thinking and acting) that needs to take place.

Compared to the use of the other looking glasses, binoculars may not be worn for as long a duration. Instead, it is more likely that binoculars looking will be performed episodically.

Binoculars looking typically offers benefits in the beginning, the middle, and end of any observational exploration:

- In the beginning of your observations, binoculars serve to identify what should be examined at greater length with other looking glasses.

- In the middle of looking, binoculars can function as a feedback loop to inform how you are approaching the use of other looking glasses.

- At the end, binoculars serve as a tollgate, to check if you should move on, or to see if something has been missed or neglected that may require further exploration.

☀ 8 ☀

KEEPING A DISTANCE

Years ago, all football coaches stood on the sidelines while calling plays and making player substitutions. Today, most every high school and college team—not just the professionals—have assistant coaches up in the booth, far removed from the immediate action, so they can better see the game, decide what plays to call, and make any necessary adjustments to the game plan. This binoculars looking from above drives the thinking and action that ensues below.

Very simply, these coaches see things from a distance they would not and cannot see when up close.

Similarly, only when seated in the grandstands can one see the patterns being formed by a marching band during its halftime performance at a football game. For example, at field level The Ohio State University Marching Band's scripting of the word "Ohio" looks like some sort of jumbled mess; the i-dotting finale by the high-stepping drum major and tuba player just looks like two band members scurrying away from the rest of the corps. But from a distant elevation, the looping and dotting testify to the ensemble's reputation as "The Best Damn Band in the Land."

Binoculars won't function if what you're viewing is too close at hand. Everything becomes a blur, and you end up seeing nothing. So, to avoid getting too close when looking with binoculars, follow these guidelines:

- Concentrate on looking at those things that are farther away, versus nearer.

- Find a high point (or alternatively, stay along the periphery) of any place.

• Position yourself so nothing blocks your full range of view.

When engaging in binoculars looking, don't sweep across the scene so rapidly that nothing in particular comes into focus. In this sense, going too fast is like being too close—both defeat the purpose of binoculars looking by failing to bring the big picture into view.

Binoculars looking should not feel like watching racecars zoom around a track; it should feel more like strolling by cars exhibited at an auto museum. You're not looking to scrutinize each car in every detail. Instead, you're looking to identify the variety of models present in the collection.

The proper use of binoculars requires scanning the horizon, taking time to notice things in view, and then continuing the scan as one (then another, and yet another) object is similarly identified. We mistakenly associate focused attention only with looking up close and in detail. Not so! Binoculars looking involves similar concentration. It also requires attentiveness. It's just being attentive at a distance. Rather than fixing attention on a single object, binoculars looking notices all of the objects that can be later examined at greater length. Its function is to see everything that is out there.

One way to perform this kind of surveying and scanning is to employ a technique commonly used by hunters when trying to locate wild game: the grid pattern method. Mentally picture a grid pattern across the horizon, imagining a dozen or so sections arrayed from left to right. Start at the leftmost section and within it, scan from top to bottom in that area. Then move from left to right and survey the next section, again scanning from top to bottom. Try to "overlap" sections with each move to the next area. In each section, look richly and thoroughly for every object present within the gridded frame. Quickly note everything that sticks out as significant.

Keeping a distance is particularly important if you are observing the behavior of people. Like a hunter stalking prey, you don't want to "spook" your target.

Keeping a distance is often useful when beginning any observation effort. It helps to identify everything that may be worthy of further examination (via other looking glasses). Keeping a distance is also important when using binoculars in the middle or end of observing. As evidenced by my golf buddies, it is hard to scan or rescan the situation when standing right atop the subject matter being studied.

✳ 9 ✳

PICKING A VANTAGE POINT

The Swiss artist Felice Varini is known for his projector-stencil technique for painting circles, squares, and lines in various urban environments—on, in, or between multiple buildings or building fixtures. The geometric shapes he paints can only be recognized by finding the one location from which the pattern can be seen. If you stand anywhere else, you will only see disaggregated fragments of paint.

Appreciating Varini's art requires binoculars looking. Each work must be taken in from a distance. One cannot stand immediately before any component fragment, as one would normally behold a framed painting. Instead, the very positioning of the onlooker serves to frame the painting. The art patron must move about to find the only vantage point from which to view the overall work. Both in and out of alignment, it is the interplay with the component pieces that enriches the art experience.

Any distance is defined by two end points. With binoculars looking, what is "out there" defines the one end, and the positioning of the looker defines the other. It is not enough to merely keep a distance when looking with binoculars; moving about to locate a suitable vantage point from which to scan the scene is also necessary.

An ideal vantage point is that place or position that affords the broadest possible perspective on what is being surveyed. Such places need to be discovered. Interestingly, Varini does not mark the place from which the fragments align; the vantage point must be discovered by interacting with the space. So it is with any environment, object, or event that you wish to survey with binoculars looking. How are such vantage points discovered?

By looking while moving about, exploring, and experimenting to pick a place that affords the widest possible view of everything to be seen. Two approaches aid in picking a vantage point for binoculars looking:

1. When surveying and scanning across inside spaces: Walk the walls. That is, navigate around the entire perimeter of the place and constantly look across to the other side of the environment.

2. When surveying and scanning across outside expanses: Head for the hills. In other words, find an elevated position for looking all around the place.

As with interacting with a Varini installation, binoculars looking does not occur only after an advantageous vantage point has been found. Instead, the binoculars looking occurs throughout the process of moving about trying to locate a vantage point. Moving itself while looking is part of binoculars use.

There are other approaches that may aid in picking a good vantage point. Many years ago, I went to see a Major League Baseball game at the Houston Astrodome. It was my first time there and I was as eager to take in the facility as I was to watch the Astros play. I went up to the ticket office and purchased a seat in the mezzanine section. This proved a big mistake: When I got to my seat I discovered that the mezzanine was located directly under the upper ring of seats. I could not see the domed ceiling from my ticketed location! I would have been better off—binocularly and financially—buying a cheap seat in the upper section of the stadium. It took less than an inning for me to realize my blunder, and I promptly relocated to the upper deck. Once up there, I walked around and tested the view from several sections before settling into my eventual seat.

I could have found this more advantageous vantage point by either consulting a stadium seating chart, or asking the ticket agent where best to take in the whole domed place. This episode suggests a third and fourth way to help locate a vantage point:

3. Consult a map, to first get an overview, and

4. Ask someone who has greater familiarity with the place in view.

⁜ 10 ⁜

WHAT DOES BINOCULARS LOOKING LOOK LIKE?

Have you ever been on a road trip and come across a sign reading "Scenic Overlook?" The sign serves as a marker calling attention to a stop-worthy place for taking in a roadside view. It tells drivers that a good vantage point exists from some particular vista. And the sign is there, because someone has already done the binoculars looking to discover this exact position.

Binoculars looking should feel like discovering such scenic overlooks. In binoculars looking you simultaneously assume a vantage point and notice a scene worth taking more time to survey.

Following are some examples of binoculars looking:

A keynote speaker for a conference in Vancouver, British Columbia, shared with meeting organizers the speaker's plans to explore the city on his own before the next day's talk. The downtown council for the city got wind of this and wanted to make sure the visiting keynoter had an opportunity to survey Vancouver from a distance before hitting the streets. So immediately after arriving by commercial airline flight, the speaker was whisked off for a private helicopter tour of the entire metropolitan area, complete with a guide pointing out various neighborhoods and landmarks. That's what binoculars looking looks like: *It provides a big picture overview for whatever looking is to follow.*

A design firm wants to identify new merchandising and display concepts for one of its major retail clients. Its designers visit Las Vegas and trek the entire length of the Strip, surveying the hotel registration lobbies and indoor shopping corridors of every hotel-casino resort in order to identify locations worth revisiting to study in greater detail. That's what binoculars looking looks like: *It scans all options before committing to examining any one in more depth.*

A tourist with limited time to take in an art museum grabs and scans a facility map, then surveys each special exhibit and permanent installations before deciding where to circle back to spend more time. That's what binoculars looking looks like: *It helps set priorities for the overall effort.*

When recruiting college seniors for potential employment after graduation, a major corporation in Cincinnati takes new hires to the observation deck of Carew Tower to point out the various residential options for living along the Ohio River (both in Ohio and in Kentucky) as well as the "mounts" that comprise the "City of Seven Hills." That's what binoculars looking looks like: *It puts different pieces into a discriminating perspective.*

A student doing fieldwork for a research paper on the funeral industry maps out a drive connecting the five largest funeral homes in town. In making the circuit, the student notices the proximity of flower shops and churches to the funeral homes. As a result, florists and pastors are added to the list of people to interview (in addition to the funeral directors previously identified). That's what binoculars looking looks like: *It helps identify thought experiments and action steps that might otherwise be missed.*

A film crew makes an advance visit to a city to find a location for shooting a key movie scene. They scan the urban environment to locate the ideal vantage point from which to shoot the footage. During the actual shoot, they survey the location to make sure no one from the general public somehow strays into the background of the scene. As the filming effort concludes, the crew scans the horizon for any extra B-roll footage they might want to capture before packing up. That's what binoculars looking looks like: *It scans across the landscape in the beginning, middle, and end of an observational mission.*

✳ 11 ✳

BINOCULARS EXERCISES

A t this point, you should understand the nature of binoculars looking pretty clearly. But understanding binoculars looking is just a first step in knowing how to skillfully look with binoculars. To further assist in the skill of looking with binoculars, practice any or all of these exercises.

COFFEE SHOP CANVASSING

Go to a nearby coffee shop, preferably one you frequent with some regularity. Before entering, let your feet do some looking by walking around the outside of the café. Survey the surroundings. Then pick a vantage point to observe arriving customers. Scan for ways people approach and step inside. Look for different behaviors. Don't focus on any one person or peculiarity for too long. Now ask yourself: Have you noticed anything that you never noticed before?

Then enter the café. Get in line and scan the scene. Repeat after each step forward. Order a drink. As you wait for your beverage, scan all around. Before taking a seat, do some more binoculars looking by walking about the entire perimeter of the café, seeking the ideal vantage point to continue binoculars looking while seated. Consider what you would see from each chair. Take an open seat, but only after surveying all of your options.

While you enjoy your drink, continue to survey the place, the people, and the entire ordering process. Don't stare. Instead, do all your looking inconspicuously. Use the grid pattern method to scan for anything that stands out in the room. Listen for the types of conversations that rise above the din, without listening to the details of any particular discussion. Then ask yourself: Have you noticed anything that you had not noticed before?

When you finish your drink, go ahead and leave. As you depart, scan for anything you might have missed when entering the place. Once outside, pick a vantage point for observing other customers, but this time observe those leaving the place. Ask yourself once more: Have you noticed anything that you never noticed before?

MONUMENTAL SNAPSHOTTING

This binoculars exercise will be described using the Lincoln Memorial on the National Mall in Washington, DC, as the object of observation. If in another city, select as famous a landmark as possible, preferably one often depicted on postcards. If you're in a town lacking such an object, trek to a nearby city that does.

Take a camera or smartphone for your visit. When you arrive, spend some time surveying and scanning the entire monument from a distance. Then move a little closer to survey and scan the exterior steps, columns, and facings. After that, move inside—remembering that you are still doing binoculars looking—to survey the statue and scan (not read) the carved inscriptions.

Always move at the periphery of the immediate scene. The entire purpose of this binoculars looking is to identify the one vantage point from which you wish to take a single photographic image. You get to take one and only one shot to capture the essence of the memorial. There are no do-overs. So take your time with your binoculars looking to richly examine the monument. Then decide what to include and not include as you frame your shot. Ask yourself: What one position lends itself to take the most compelling photograph?

Later, print and frame your photograph and decide (first using binoculars, of course!) where to display it in your home or office.

Note: If you perform this exercise with others as a group, be sure each person works independently. Once all have taken a photo, put all of them into a single slideshow presentation as a survey of the various vantage points.

Afterward, look at postcards of the Lincoln Memorial and compare your photograph(s) with those sold to typical (non-binoculars using) tourists. Which do you like better and why?

MAGAZINE RACK-A-TOURING

Go to a magazine rack. (Really good ones are increasingly hard to find, but try a major bookstore, or if all else fails, visit an airport concessioner.) Go on a binoculars tour of the displayed magazines.

First, stand back and pick a vantage point to observe how various customers go about browsing the various selections.

Then step closer and survey all the different categories and subcategories of magazines, slowly walking the full length of the display. Be sure to keep a safe distance—more than one arm-length away—so you cannot reach out and grab any of the magazines.

Circle again, scanning for any magazine titles, cover art, or other magazine characteristics that jump out at you. Don't overly read any covers. (Remember, you're doing binoculars looking, not comprehensive reading.) Instead, scan for what titles strike you as new and unusual, or usual yet intriguing.

Note that every magazine title is targeted at some human interest, and then ask yourself: With what previously unfamiliar human interests or consumer behaviors have you now become more interested?

Once done using binoculars to survey the entire magazine rack, go ahead a grab a copy of the magazine that most intrigues you. Try to avoid just picking out something of personal interest that you would usually select, and instead pick some new discovery that you've uncovered.

Now perform binoculars looking with that magazine! Don't read it, instead survey and scan the issue—first its front and back covers, then any inserts, and finally the advertising and content. Keep a distance from the actual articles or ad copy. (Again, you are looking more than reading.) Then ask yourself: With what previously unfamiliar subject matter or consumer behavior have you now become even more interested?

Now, are you going to buy that magazine?

12

SUMMARY OF
BINOCULARS LOOKING

Looking with binoculars is one of Six Looking Glasses available to wear at any moment to enhance your observational prowess. Before moving on to study the remaining five looking glasses, let's take a step back and recap some of the major attributes of binoculars looking. With binoculars you

- look across any scene, surrounding, or circumstance,

- survey and scan your environment,

- seek to see the "big picture,"

- establish an overall context for other types of looking,

- orient yourself (or your group) as an active looker(s),

- avoid jumping to conclusions or acting too hastily,

- keep a distance from the observed scene,

- pick a vantage point from which to avail yourself of the widest array of areas and elements within the environment,

- look while moving about to find a place to be best positioned,

- repeat scanning and surveying, at the beginning, middle, and end of the overall observational effort (interspersed with use of other looking glasses),

- move in a grid-like pattern as a set of mental frames across the horizon, and

- set priorities for the use of other looking glasses.

In short, you can use binoculars looking whenever first entering a new environment, when circumstances have changed within that environment, or if time is limited.

Having looked with binoculars, let's consider what other looking glasses would be suitable to do further observational exploration.

BIFOCALS LOOKING

≡ Let's compare what it looks like from opposite ends of the room.

≡ It does look impressive at night, but we should return to see it during the day.

≡ Contrast the big ones on the shelf with the smaller versions behind the counter.

≡ We should watch how the children react with and without supervision.

A number of students of nearly equal ability were in the same mathematics course. For homework their teacher assigned all the odd-numbered problems at the back of each chapter in the textbook. This continued week after week as the class made its way through all the material.

Occasional quizzes were administered by the teacher, with problems that differed from the ones assigned as homework. The students perform with mixed success; but one student did particularly well, far exceeding the performance of all others in the class.

Starting with the very first homework assignment, in addition to doing the assigned problems this student also looked at the unassigned ones at the back of each chapter—and then after the first quiz, started to solve the even-numbered problems as well, despite not being required to do so. This continued throughout the semester, each and every week, solving both the odd- and even-numbered problems.

This student's success was due to bifocals looking—by looking at an opposite set of problems from the required set. Now, you might say that looking at this opposite set of questions had little to do with the student's performance; it was just the additional practice that really helped. Well, you might think that until learning that the teacher used the even-numbered problems in the textbook to create all the quizzes. This one student alone noticed this fact—and didn't tell his fellow students!

⁂ 13 ⁂

LOOKING BETWEEN:
COMPARING AND CONTRASTING

No one has ever really designed an automobile for a woman. There is no good place to put a purse. Why has no car company yet created a purse compartment? Because they haven't done bifocals looking to compare and contrast how differently men and women typically enter and settle into their vehicles.

Nor has anyone has ever specifically designed a car for a dog: there is no separate door, with a pullout ramp—like some delivery trucks utilize—to allow dogs (especially tiny and/or old ones) to get in without having to jump. Why has no car company thought to design an automobile for dog owners, especially when they are known to spend lavishly on their pets? Because they haven't looked at the difference between how humans and dogs enter cars, and, just as important, they haven't noticed how dog owners and non-dog owners differently treat their vehicles.

Car makers have designed vehicles for adults with children: witness the minivan. But have they then gone on to look—with bifocals—at how families without a minivan cope? Some couples I know have made pacts to never allow one partner to convince the other to buy a minivan. Bifocals looking between how van-willing and van-averse parents use their vehicles might lead to offering more van-like features in non-van vehicles (and visa-versa).

One car manufacturer has introduced a foot-activated trunk release for people carrying bags of groceries or other bulky items. The mechanism frees up arms and hands to load and unload goods from the vehicle without fiddling with handles and keys. But has this automobile company then gone on to also look—with bifocals—at grocery shoppers using plastic versus paper bags? Or has it done bifocals looking at those using reusable bags in lieu of paper or plastic? Such bifocals looking might uncover ways to stop shopping bags from rattling around the trunk after being loaded!

For any given situation there exists a host of different dimensions of the scene that can be compared and contrasted as an act of looking. This is the very essence of bifocals looking: pairing two alternative views of a scene and then looking at the difference between the two in a reciprocal oscillating action.

The process is: (1) pick a paired set of views, and then (2) look with one view and then the other to compare and contrast what you see.

We usually just think of bifocals as allowing separate looks of far and near. Indeed, this is the set of views paired in an actual pair of physical bifocals. But as a looking metaphor, bifocals should be understood as allowing the wearer to readily transition between any primary view to another secondary view. As one of the Six Looking Glasses, bifocals consist of pairing any two views as a single looking instrument aimed at gaining a more informed look at a scene. (Bifocals looking, in a sense, combines two lenses as a single bifurcated viewfinder.)

Some bifocals combinations can include: male/female, human/dog, parent/child, even/odd, or a host of other possibilities. These unique pairings work to enhance the observing.

What is the value of bifocals looking? First and foremost, the use of bifocals helps overcome the human tendency to only see that which confirms preexisting notions about any subject or particular object of attention— what psychologists call confirmation bias. Bifocals force an acknowledgment of this propensity, making the observer consciously and deliberately choose to couple one's preconceived view with a different, juxtaposed view. If car designers are biased toward only seeing male interaction with vehicles, effort must be made to also observe female patterns of behavior. If attention is only placed on how humans interact with an environment, the interactions of their pet animals might also be observed.

Useful insights often flow from such polarized observations. If a play center is looking for ways to enhance its overall experience, management should not only watch how children play, but also how their parents watch their kids play. If only odd-numbered problems are assigned by a teacher, students should also look at the even-numbered ones.

Bifocals looking requires formally pairing two such views to compare and contrast different aspects of what is there to see. The key lies in experimenting with various alternative pairings. Choose different pairings to create—in a sense—altogether different pairs of bifocals.

This is the main difference between bifocals looking and all the other looking glasses. No such switching of viewpoints *within* the specific looking function occurs with the use of any of the other types of looking glasses. But with bifocals, this use of different and multiple pairings of views—as part of the very use of the looking glass itself—is critical to its proper function and use.

Finally, remember that the purpose of bifocals looking is to escape the paradigms that usually dominate our observational gaze. Bifocals provide a means of seeing noteworthy anomalies in the scene that we would otherwise not notice. Bifocals looking, in fact, should itself be treated as an anomaly from normal looking—forcing peculiar, irregular, and uncommon comparisons.

Note: The point of this comparing and contrasting with bifocals is not to yield yet more contrasting comparisons (although seeing more of them might occur), but to find some comparison that yields a discovery that would not have been seen without taking the time to contrast looking at something one way and then another. Indeed, the whole point of bifocals (here, similar to any other looking glass) is to make observations that might trigger some new thought and excite some subsequent action.

Use bifocals looking whenever you catch yourself instinctively looking with an all-too-comfortable perspective in all-too-automatic manner. This practice will help you break that pattern by intentionally looking from a paired perspective.

14

PAIRING OPPOSITES

Ever notice a door with the words "Push" or "Pull" on it? The posted instructions are only needed because the door cues users to interact with it in a manner completely counter to the way it opens—with some handle to be pushed, or a crossbar to be pulled. Seeing the Push/Pull calls attention to the muddled messaging, not only pointing to the need for better door-opening cues, but also suggesting a more general conclusion, namely that all posted text as instructional signage is an indication of poor design.

Let's now generalize and apply this realization to make an even broader point, namely, that all articulated pairings of opposites can help you see some design improvements that might otherwise be overlooked.

Bifocals looking begins with the identification of pairing of opposites. How then can such pairings be created or identified?

The easiest way is simply to first identify the one way you are already looking. Then pair it with another way. For example, if you are looking at chocolate candy bars, also look at non-chocolate bars. Or look at candy bars and non-candy bars as a pairing. Be playful in creating pairings. You never know what new discoveries might follow.

Another straightforward means to generate pairing possibilities involves the journalistic line of inquiry—asking Who, What, Where, When, Why and How—as prompts for coming up with contrasting views to compare.

For example, you might use any of these opposite pairings for bifocals looking:

WHO	WHAT	WHERE
Male/Female	Big/Small	Top/Bottom
Adult/Child	Tall/Short	Left/Right
Younger/Older	Thick/Thin	Front/Back
Single/Couple	Natural/Artificial	Inside/Outside
Individual/Group	Original/Imitation	Center/Periphery
Familiar/Unfamiliar	Common/Uncommon	Separate/Together

WHEN	WHY	HOW
Before/After	More/Less	Color/Black-and-White
Morning/Afternoon	Empty/Full	Noisy/Quiet
Day/Night	Open/Closed	Hard/Soft
Earlier/Later	On/Off	Warm/Cold
Arriving/Departing	First/Last	Many/Few
Frequent/Infrequent	Used/Unused	Even/Odd

These pairings were generated by asking the following questions: Who might be oppositely paired? What might be oppositely paired? Where might opposite pairs be located? When might opposites occur? Why might opposites happen? How might opposites be paired?

You might have come up with an entirely different set of pairings under these six headings. That's fine. The categories are only presented here as one list of possibilities. Feel free to come up with other pairings to use.

Regardless of the pairings chosen, bifocals looking requires seeing things "both ways" or "like this and like that." It offers a way of seeing what would otherwise be missed when only looking in one particular manner.

✳ 15 ✳

ALTERING DIRECTIONS

A t this point you might be thinking that bifocals looking is antonym-looking and understandably so. For many pairings of lenses using bifocals will often involve the use of directly opposite views of a given situation. But in selecting contrasting lenses, the contrast need not be so stark.

Let's consider the use of a compass to explain. There are any number of directions you can face when using a compass. For example, you can face north, then south. You can face east, then west. You can even face northeast, then southwest and then face southeast, then northwest. All are directly opposite directions: N/S, E/W, NE/SW, SE/NW. But you could also choose to face north and then east, south and then northwest. While not directly opposite pairings, each represents an opposing pair of views. The two different directions are placed in opposition to each other. They are treated as opposites.

Facing in one direction and then another is akin to looking in one direction and then another. First you face a certain direction to then look in that direction. With bifocals looking, you actually choose to face and look in two different directions. Sometimes these directions are direct opposites; sometimes they are not. But even when not directly opposite directions, the two views are still treated as opposing ones.

To illustrate, let's take a half-dozen of the journalist pairings found in the previous chapter and come up with a few new (and opposing) alternatives:

- Besides before/after, try before/during.
- Besides morning/afternoon, try afternoon/at-noon.
- Besides more/less, try less/none.

◆ Besides open/closed, try open/half-open.

◆ Besides color/black-and-white, try one-color/multi-color.

◆ In lieu of warm/cold, try warm/lukewarm.

There is virtually no limit to the pairings you can create. Let's change direction now and look at the one pairing most associated with an actual pair of bifocals. What would that pairing be? What particularly unique behavior is most evident when using bifocals? It's looking up and then looking down, of course. Someone wearing bifocals may sit reading the newspaper, looking down at the pages; that person might then look up to check the time on a clock.

Up then down. Down then up.

More importantly, this one up-and-down movement of the eyes is coupled with going back and forth. Bifocals looking always involves looking back and forth between each lens. Regardless of the particular set of lenses being paired as bifocals, the looking alternates, comparing and contrasting what is seen in different directions, forcing new patterns of observation.

Think of the use of bifocals as a game of ping-pong. The two paddles represent the two bifocal lenses, paired for the game. With each volley, the two lenses go back and forth in different directions, aimed up and down at varying heights. When one volley concludes, another begins. And the ball never bounces back and forth in exactly the same path.

Now let's press the analogy, and modify the game a little bit. After every so many volleys, both paddles are exchanged for a new set: blue/red smooth rubber paddles are replaced with light-green/dark-green pimpled rubber ones; then after a few more volleys, one of these paddles is exchanged for a spongy anti-topspin one. After a few more volleys, the other is exchanged for a cork paddle (yes, there are cork-surfaced ping-pong paddles).

This would make for a rather unusual game of ping-pong. But such playfulness is precisely what you want with bifocals: For any set of paddles (lenses), the volley (paired looking) alternates back and forth between the two. And with each paddle (lens), each hit (view) is made at a different direction with that paddle (lens). Then a new set of paddles (lenses) are used to look yet again.

✳ 16 ✳

WHAT DOES BIFOCALS
LOOKING LOOK LIKE?

Recall how binoculars looking calls for periodically taking in the big picture, to help determine which of the other looking glasses might be useful to next use. In a similar way, bifocals can help direct the use of other looking glasses. When approaching any object or area of attention, bifocals are good to use before going on to make more detailed observations with magnifying-glass looking or microscope looking, or to enhance your view with rose-colored looking or blindfold looking, or even to go back for more binoculars looking.

What did your parents say to do before crossing the street? Look both ways! Following are some examples of "looking both ways" with bifocals:

A high school football coach diligently studies each week's game film to prepare his players for the next contest. This footage (filmed from a binoculars perspective) always reveals mistakes made during the previous game. When the same film is reviewed with players, the coach does not just point out mistakes and what should have been done. Instead, he asks each player what it looked like in the moment from the field, why they did what they did. That's what bifocals looking looks like: *It pairs one perspective with another to get a fuller picture of what's to be seen.*

A project team for a fast food chain seeks to find ways to speed up drive-through lines. While studying ordering inefficiencies, the team decides to look at cars with solo drivers paired against those with passengers. They also look at multi-passenger cars with just adults versus those with adults and children. They look at two-door vehicles versus four-door vehicles.

They look during lunch and dinner hours. They pit weekends against weekdays. They compare and contrast behaviors on sunny days versus days it rains or snows. That's what bifocals looking looks like: *It identifies myriad new combinations for examining any particular problem.*

The design team for a new hotel resort wants to think more creatively about the layout for swimming pools and poolside amenities. Before any ideation or sketch work, the group invests in watching swimmers at other existing resorts. They watch early morning exercisers as well as afternoon sunbathers. They watch sunbathers with and without reading material. They contrast those who read from bound books versus those using electronic tablets. They watch those who eat and drink, versus those who don't. They watch those who order drinks versus those who bring their own beverages. They watch those who take floatable items into the pool versus those who don't. They watch people who put their sandals neatly under their chaise lounges versus those who haphazardly toss them aside. That's what bifocals looking looks like: *It forces consideration of additional features and functionality.*

A geography student takes hold of a roadmap and holds it right side up. After a quick study of the main boundary lines, the student turns it upside down to see what the borders of the place (be it California, the United States, North America, the Americas, or the world) look like from this opposite perspective. That's what bifocals looking looks like: *It takes the initiative to take a second opposing view of the object being examined.*

After a wedding reception, the groom and groomsmen change into their street clothes. They gather all the rented tuxedos, shoes, shirts, ties, and so forth to be returned the next day. But one cummerbund has gone missing. Rather than frantically searching the entire room for where it might be, they first decide to look both on everyone as well as off. By looking on each other, they immediately find the missing article curled up around the waist of the groom's father! That's what bifocals looking looks like: *It considers the non-obvious.*

A graphic designer mocks up a layout for a client's brochure, pairing various colors, fonts, and artwork—one way, then another, and yet another—testing different combinations: this color with that font; this font with that icon; placed on this side versus that edge. That's what bifocals looking looks like: *It experiments with various contrasting views and compares the differences.*

✳ 17 ✳

BIFOCALS EXERCISES

Following are three exercises, each designed to practice a particular aspect of bifocals looking. The first involves the skill of creating pairings. The second assigns pairings to practice alternating between opposing views. The third combines both aspects in a final bifocals drill comparing and contrasting.

GROCERIES-PAIRING

Go visit your favorite grocery store. Grab a cart. Enter the aisles and go grocery shopping.

As soon as you can, grab an item at random, any item, and place it in the top shelf of the cart. Then proceed farther down the aisle and locate a second item to pair with the first, grab it, and also place it in the top part of the cart. Be sure to select some underlying criterion for this pairing of two items. For example, if the first random item was a small can of soup, perhaps grab a large can of soup—utilizing a small/large pairing.

Then locate another item to replace one of the two in the cart. Place the substitute item in the top shelf and put the replaced item in the lower, larger basket. Again, use some underlying criterion to create this new pairing. For example, a box of spices might replace the large can of soup—for a can/box pairing.

Keep this up as you proceed through each aisle. Make as many substitutions as you can, one at a time, creating a new pairing with each successive item selected. Try to pair obvious opposites but also create opposing pairings that may not be so obvious. The goal is to identify as many pairings as possible. (Your success will be visibly demonstrated by how full your lower basket becomes.)

After making your way through all the aisles, ask yourself: What techniques did you use to identify the various pairings? (Then, if you don't want to buy all this stuff, find some opposing ways to deal with the now full cart. For example: Buy cart/abandon cart, or place items back on proper shelves/place items on random shelves.)

CEREAL BOX FLIPPING

Try this one at home. Go to the kitchen cupboard or pantry and grab a box of cereal. Then sit down at the table and place the box in front of you.

Before starting, remember that you're not doing magnifying-glass or microscope looking. If at any time you sense yourself examining the details of the box, flip it to the reverse side. Avoid focusing on some one feature, or shifting from one detail to another on the same side of the box. Be disciplined: Bounce between one side of the box to the other—only to compare and contrast elements of the packaging found on different sides of the cereal box.

Begin with comparing front and back sides of the box. Look for how various design elements are presented: fonts, artwork, logos, colors, and so forth. Notice differences between the two sides. Look for what is on one side but altogether missing on the other. Flip back and forth.

Now do the same flipping—and noticing—between the box top and bottom. Look for how the same elements may be presented differently and look for new elements to compare. Keep flipping and keep looking.

Next, flip between the left and right panels of the box. Look for yet more contrasting elements of the packaging. Flip and look. Flip and look.

Can you guess the final pairing? Open the box and take out the inner bag. Use bifocals to compare and contrast the box with the bag. Look at box and then the bag; look at the bag and then the box. What did you discover?

Here are some of the contrasts that I noticed on a box of Wheaties:

- Front/back: size of font; number of pictures, overall "busyness," picture atop text vs. text atop picture; multiple website addresses vs. none

- Top/bottom: use-by date vs. barcode; photographer acknowledgement on bottom vs. none

- Left/right: Nutritional facts vs. player stats

- Bag/box: transparent vs. opaque

Two features really jumped out at me: (1) the fact that the cereal flakes could be seen in the bag, but not the bag in the box, and (2) the fact that photographer acknowledgments were printed on the bottom of the box.

These key observations triggered two new thoughts: (1) creating a transparent cereal box, or a portion of the box, with artwork and graphics printed on the inner bag—if only as a promotional item, or as a special commemorative box, and (2) acknowledging, perhaps on the back of the box, the history of the Wheaties logo—who first created it, how it evolved over time, why it is designed the way it is.

After your bifocals looking, ask yourself: What features did you see that you never noticed before? Do any strike you as particularly interesting? And does any of this looking trigger some new thinking?

ROOM-INATING

This exercise—to be performed indoors—asks you to both come up with bifocals pairings on your own and then use them to look.

Leave the room you are presently occupying and go to another. Before donning bifocals, do some binoculars looking to pick a vantage point from which to be positioned for the rest of the exercise. Find the best position to take in the new room.

Once you've found your post, first use these pairings: ceiling/floor, front-wall/back-wall, left-wall/right-wall. Note what you see.

After doing this looking, identify three new pairings of your own. Make each selection of lenses an obviously opposite pairing. Then do bifocals looking with each of these three pairings of lenses, one set at a time.

Next, come up with yet three more pairings, only this time come up with non-obvious dimensions that you place in opposition to each other. Once you have these identified, do bifocals looking with each pairing.

When done, ask yourself: What did you see? Did you make any interesting observations? Did these trigger any new thoughts? Are you now wanting to change something in the room?

Finally, feel free to move to another room and repeat the exercise to practice further.

✳ **18** ✳

SUMMARY OF BIFOCALS LOOKING

W e now have a pair of looking glasses in our toolkit, having examined both binoculars looking and bifocals looking. Before moving to the next looking glass, let's compare and contrast these two different ways of looking. It's a fitting way to recap what we've learned thus far:

- Binoculars look across a scene; bifocals look between two different dimensions within the scene.

- Binoculars survey and scan; bifocals compare and contrast.

- Binoculars look at the "big picture"; bifocals pair opposing views.

- Binoculars establish context; bifocals create additional contexts.

- Binoculars orient the looker; bifocals offer an escape, challenging the looker's normal observation-making orientation.

- Binoculars slow down looking; bifocals split the looking.

- Binoculars require you to oscillate; bifocals require you to bifurcate.

- Binoculars keep a distance in order to view; bifocals always keep a comparison in view.

- Binoculars pick a vantage point to take as a position; bifocals place alternative points of view in opposing position.

- Binoculars benefit from repeated use at the beginning, middle, and end of an observational effort; bifocals benefit from experimenting with different sets of juxtaposed lenses throughout the observational time.

- The use of binoculars often moves in a grid-like pattern; the use of bifocals ping-pongs back and forth between lenses.

- Binoculars set observation priorities; bifocals find anomalies (worthy of attention) that might otherwise be overlooked.

Use bifocals whenever you sense you are missing something. Recognize the dominant way you are viewing something and pair it with opposing views to get the rest of the picture.

MAGNIFYING-GLASS LOOKING

≡ Let's stop and look at this one feature in more detail.

≡ What is most significant about this? Let's pinpoint the main point.

≡ We need to take a closer look. Let's see what pulls everything together.

≡ I know the place is busy, but we need to spot the reason for its appeal.

The Forum Shops in Las Vegas, adjacent to Caesar's Palace, generates higher sales per square foot than any other retail shopping mall. As such, it's an iconic venue for understanding contemporary consumer behavior. Its themed streetscape, meandering mix of retail shops, spiral escalators, artificial clouds in an arched ceiling, and animatronic fountain shows continue to attract shoppers year after year. When in Vegas I usually visit the place, hoping to find some new discovery about what contributes to the place's success.

One time my business partner and I were walking about the Shops when I suddenly stopped and said, "Joe, look." I pointed to a waist-high funnel about five feet in diameter, located in the middle of the corridor, into which shoppers could dispense coins and watch them spiral around and around until dropping into a hole at the bottom. Behind it stood a sign stating that all the funneled coins were donated to a charity. "Yeah?" Joe replied. He didn't immediately catch on.

So I explained (having quickly transitioned from looking to thinking to speaking): For anyone deriving any level of satisfaction watching the coin spiral, the giving no longer represented an act of pure charity. I had spotted the significance: The coin-spiraling device represented a form of narcithropy— giving in order to get some experience for oneself.

The term *narcithropy* came to me because I had first done magnifying-glass looking to pinpoint something of significance. In a mall full of objects, I had zeroed in on the one main thing really worth zeroing in on.

⁂ 19 ⁑

LOOKING CLOSER:
PAUSING AND PINPOINTING

What is your memory of first using a magnifying glass? Perhaps you remember sitting on the front sidewalk or back porch as a youngster and using a magnifying glass to burn a hole through a sheet of paper or to fry an ant—fascinated with how you could direct the sunlight into a narrow beam to penetrate the paper or zap the ant.

Of course, using a magnifying glass to burn a hole in a sheet of paper or to fry an ant is not the intended use of the instrument. But even this secondary use of a magnifying glass demonstrates the key characteristic found with its primary use: to look more closely at something. Just as the magnifying glass can be used to intensify the sun's rays, so it is used to intensify one's looking. The looking becomes directed, like a beam, onto a single aspect of whatever is being observed. You look more closely because you concentrate on just one feature of some object, one element of some process, or one dimension in some place.

This magnifying-glass looking is thus pinpointed looking.

To pinpoint looking, you must first pause—taking a firm grip of the magnifying glass—to allow for an extended look at the one feature, element, or dimension to be examined. Just as no hole will ever burn through the paper if you fail to hold the instrument absolutely steady, no insight will be gleaned from magnifying-glass looking without first pausing to place singular attention on a target.

Unlike the surveying and scanning performed with binoculars, or the comparing and contrasting inherent to bifocals, the use of magnifying-glass looking requires refraining from such vacillating activity in order to fix attention toward one point, and just one point. For some extended period of time the looking must be directed at a single object of attention.

With magnifying-glass looking there must be this moment of pausing, when all the looking converges upon one thing. This pause allows for sustained concentration. It's the pause before the formal pinpointing.

Let's liken this magnifying-glass looking—pausing and pinpointing—to threading a needle. To accomplish the task, you must pause, focus attention, and concentrate on just one spot—the hole in the needle. Imagine trying to accomplish such needle threading without this pause. Even someone exceptionally skilled in needlepoint must make this pause, however briefly.

The point, of course, is not just to pause, but to pause in order to locate the one main detail worth examining further.

This pinpointed looking entails closer looking.

Recall how with binoculars you must find a vantage point from which to survey and scan. With magnifying-glass looking you must find a focal point upon which to concentrate looking. The result is a closer, enlarged view—a magnified view.

Try this exercise: Find the "focal point" amidst the jumble of the following letters.

f t o s d f g h h w d u j k o l f s g s g s h j u I o p p d s s e d

d b h j k t y u x g k o e s h j k y f s c g k h j l y g s s d s s f

f f j j y y s z s z y z f o c a l p o i n t x c x c g h i i g g b b i

d f g u i o p d w q w e r t y j b f s i h f g h k c f g h j d s v i

y o z a r f s o s o f g x j i i v j d v b h j k i u o p s r f b o v e

Okay, pause and try again.

f t o s d f g h h w d u j k o l f s g s g s h j u I o p p d s s e d

d b h j k t y u x g k o e s h j k y f s c g k h j l y g s s d s s f

f f j j y y s z s z y z f o c a l p o i n t x c x c g h i g g b b i

d f g u I o p d w q w e r t y j b f s i h f g h k c f g h j d s v i

y o z a r f s o s o f g x j i i v j d v b h j k i u o p s r f b o v e

And a third time.

f t o s d f g h h w d u j k o l f s g s g s h j u I o p p d s s e d

d b h j k t y u x g k o e s h j k y f s c g k h j l y g s s d s s f

f f j j y y s z s z y z f o c a l p o i n t x c x c g h i g g b b

d f g u I o p d w q w e r t y j b f s i h f g h k c f g h j d s v i

y o u a r e s o s o f i x e d o n t h a t t h i r d l i n e a b o v e

Of course, you found the "focal point" each time (enlarging its font size surely helped). But the third go-round, did you also notice how the last line changed? You didn't? Good—that means you really concentrated on the focal point! Now go back and concentrate on the last line as a new, alternative focal point.

At the risk of belaboring the pinpoint: Choose some other letters upon which to concentrate your magnifying-glass attention. Can you spot the only "q?" (Or spot what follows it?) Or the only capitalized letter in the mix?

Of course, most any circumstance other than this contrived exercise probably represents a more meaningful occasion for someone to pinpoint items with magnifying-glass looking: a security guard eying suspicious activity; a student finding a good seat for class; a couple picking a quiet place in a park to put down their picnic blanket; a dance troupe watching how a particular move is performed when learning a difficult new dance routine; even a person readying to swat a fly.

In many circumstances, the use of magnifying-glass looking will occur after having already used binoculars: The student has already surveyed the classroom for all seating options; the couple has scanned the park for various nooks; and the dancers have reviewed the entire number top-to-bottom from start-to-finish. Or it may be used after having used bifocals: The security guard has already compared and contrasted someone's odd behavior versus normal shoppers; and the movements of the fly, here and there, have already been noted.

The reason to then switch to magnifying-glass looking is to further examine one thing in more detail: Is the seat or the nook really as desirable as it appears at a distance? What all is involved, exactly, in that one dance move? Is the suspicious activity truly cause for alarm, or not? Should the fly be struck from the left or from the right?

⁂ 20 ⁑

SPOTTING ONE MAIN POINT

Magnifying means enlarging some scene inside what's seen. It means spotting one main detail that stands out among all else in view, pinpointing that which is worth spending more time examining, and blotting everything else out. But how do you decide upon this one detail? How do you decide where to pinpoint the magnifying-glass looking in this way? How do you choose to spot this, and not that?

There are two approaches available are

1. instinctive and

2. intentional.

To spot the main point instinctively means selecting something without having any particular reason, without any preconceived intention as to why. Return for a moment to the paper-burning illustration: When using a magnifying glass to point a beam at one spot on the sheet of paper, you do not spend much time thinking about where to direct the light beam. You just pick a spot. That's spotting instinctively.

When spotting one main detail in this manner, just look for what "pops" out, and only look at what pops out. The key: Trust that your magnifying-glass looking will spontaneously spot a worthy detail, simply because you are using magnifying-glass looking. Your looking thus becomes the very act of spotting.

There is one big benefit to this approach: It helps keep the thinking out of the looking. If you think too much, or, to put it more accurately, if you think too often while using magnifying-glass looking, new discoveries may be missed. What your mind thinks of (in advance) as significant often prohibits letting your eye discover (in the moment) some new significance in the scene.

When you use magnifying-glass looking, try first to instinctively spot one main detail. The key is to trust the immediacy of the moment. Turn to the scene, look, and let yourself see: What immediately pops out from everything else? It could be anything, something, or nothing at all.

If one main detail does not become immediately apparent through this instinctive approach, try the second approach and intentionally select some criterion to help pinpoint one main detail. Any number of criteria can assist here. (This is just a way to intentionally bring to the surface the tacit reasons that lie beneath any criterion that might be selected instinctively.)

Here is a checklist using five Ns to help spot some detail:

1. *Newness*: Notice any detail that strikes you as new—new to you, new to the typical context of the scene, or new to the world.

2. *Novelty*: Look for any detail that strikes you as unfamiliar, even strange.

3. *Names*: Notice any names assigned to any aspect of what is viewed. Something that has been given a name often indicates that someone else thinks some detail important (be it that which is named, the name chosen, or the basis for selecting the name). And is there something unnamed that you notice as well?

4. *Nucleus*: Look for anything that strikes you as being central to the scene—some essential part around which all the other details are organized.

5. *Nonessential*: Notice any detail that does not fit with the rest of the scene, such as something accidental, unnecessary, or superfluous.

In a nutshell: Notice the most noticeable. Spot some color, shape, or size that stands out. Pinpoint some process, technique, or method. Pick some movement, placement, or other ordering of affairs. Be careful not to pick multiple criteria or to run through a long list of potential spot-picking cues. The intentional approach is really only meant to get you more comfortable with pinpointing some detail more instinctively.

✳ 21 ✳

FINDING THE SIGNIFICANCE

After spotting one main point, do not immediately move on to spotting more details (that would be microscope looking). Rather, take time to dwell on the significance of the one identified detail. Hold your attention on that significance and how it relates to the overall scene.

To illustrate how this can be done, let's turn to a tale of biblical proportion. In the first century AD, the apostle Paul visited Athens, Greece, where in the Christian scriptures we are told he encountered a city "full of idols." Later when Paul stood in the Areopagus and spoke before a gathering of Epicurean and Stoic philosophers, he called specific attention to just one of these idols, one that bore the inscription "To the unknown god." Of all the idols in town, when it came time to share his thoughts on what he had observed during his tour of the city, Paul highlighted this one object with his Greek audience. He had pinpointed the one detail that held the most significance, the one detail that represented the very essence of all that he had seen in the greater cityscape.

Travel and tourism have always presented opportunities to take in new sights. Some popular vacation destinations today are visited by tens of millions of people each year. At certain historical landmarks, wave after wave of visitors take in the same famously familiar attractions. How often does someone spot anything besides the obvious, see the landmark anew, and take note of something truly significant? Better tour guides at these venues—those who have accumulated a great storehouse of knowledge about the particular venue—often point visitors less familiar with the venue to some uniquely significant aspect of the site.

Consider travelers who fly a lot. These frequent fliers have become so accustomed to the same old seating and seatback setting that most could probably tell you the precise arrangement of everything there—the number and size of seat pockets; the placement of the airline magazine, merchandise catalog, and safety instruction card in the larger pocket; the folds and tabs on the airsickness bag; the location of the recessed cup circle on the tray table; the position of the recline button on the seat, and so forth. From my description here, you can probably tell that I fly a lot! So let me share the insight I gained using magnifying-glass looking one day on a flight.

It was a nearly three-hour flight on American Airlines from Cleveland Hopkins International to Dallas/Fort Worth International. After the plane had reached a "safe and comfortable cruising altitude" (frequent flyers are also most familiar with the precise language of various flight announcements), the flight attendants made their way down the aisle with the beverage cart. When it arrived at my row, I politely declined any beverage. Then the woman next to me did the same thing. We both declined "something to drink"—for a three-hour trip. For a flight of this duration, our behavior struck me as unusual, novel even.

I stopped what I was doing, paused, and deliberately looked to see if I could pinpoint what it was that triggered two side-by-side passengers to forego the offer of free beverages on the three-hour flight. I then spotted the one main point of significance, the one item that explained our beverage-declining behavior: both of us had wedged in the seat pocket in front of us, a plastic bottle of Pepsi-Cola. (I prefer Coke over Pepsi, and American Airlines serves Coca-Cola, so my purchase of Pepsi to bring onboard called further attention to the novelty of my own behavior.)

Why had the bottles of Pepsi popped out at me? What about them stood out as significantly central in explaining the scene? Both my seatmate and I had planned to use our laptops during the flight. We didn't want to spill any liquids on our computers. And we wanted to be able to cap our drink containers.

In this moment, based on this magnifying-glass identification of the two plastic bottles, it dawned on me that the entire seatback and tray-table configuration on an airplane was designed in a pre-laptop era! This observation then triggered the thought that the entire design of the beverage-drinking space, and with it the beverage-serving process, ought to be redesigned:

Airlines should hand out small bottles with caps instead of open cans and cups and integrate a bottle-holder into the armrest or seatback.

With magnifying-glass looking, you pause to pinpoint the significance of some detail. You simply pause and look until you spot the one thing worth really noticing.

✳ 22 ✳

WHAT DOES MAGNIFYING–GLASS LOOKING LOOK LIKE?

Ever notice how a young child, surrounded by dozens of toys, can become fixated on just one? Or have you ever seen a child inseparably attached to a stuffed animal or a blanket? Nothing else at the time seems to matter to the kid; the only item of significance in the entire space is that one toy, animal, or blanket.

I recall one Christmas Eve at my in-laws' home, with ten grandchildren gathered to open presents. At one point young William, age three or so, unwrapped a large package that contained dozens of small plastic animals. His parents helped remove the miniature creatures and at the very instant all of them dropped from the box, little William became interested in the empty box! No effort to direct his attention to the animals could draw his interest away from the box. He had spotted the one main item of interest. In watching this episode unfold, I spotted why he found the box so interesting: The inner and outer box components could be slid in and out of each other. The plastic animals, with no moving parts, offered no such interplay.

Magnifying-glass looking is characterized by this sudden interest in a single point of attention. Here are some additional examples of such pinpointed looking:

A sorting machine in a factory keeps jamming, shutting down the line. The line worker repeatedly clears the machine of damaged boxes, only to have the jam reoccur. Then after clearing the next (and soon to be final) jam, the worker remains stationed at the machine and waits and watches for the next jam to happen. Sure enough, the machine jams, but this time the problem is pinpointed—a bolt has become loose, bumping one type of box off-track. That's what magnifying-glass looking looks like: *It pauses to pinpoint.*

Offensive and defensive lines square off in a football game. The ball is snapped. As the two lines battle, they blur into one. The quarterback hands the ball off to his tailback. There appears to be no place for the runner to go, but he suddenly spots an opening in the line, plants his foot to make a cut (a momentary pause in his running), and darts through for a major gain in yardage. That's what magnifying-glass looking looks like: *It spots the one thing of significance amidst all other action.*

Frank Wills, a security guard in the Watergate building in Washington, DC, spots a piece of duct tape affixed to the side of the door, covering the latch plate. He removes it and continues his rounds. Later he returns to the door and again finds the latch covered by tape. He calls the police. Five burglars breaking into the Democratic National Committee headquarters housed in the building are arrested. A scandal unfolds, a president resigns, and the course of history is changed—all because Mr. Wills spots that tape. That's what magnifying-glass looking looks like: *It notices what stands out.*

A couple driving through their neighborhood notices a garage sale, spotting what appears to be an unusual piece of furniture. They stop, proceed directly to the item, and make a prolonged inspection before buying it for a low price. The item turns out to be rare and valuable. That's what magnifying-glass looking looks like: *It helps zero in to get a closer look.*

Liberty Tax hires workers during tax season to dress up as Uncle Sam or the Statue of Liberty and stand outside as wavers, hoping to draw attention to its tax preparation business. The company instructs these employees not to wave at the cars as they pass by, but to look inside the vehicles and wave to each driver. That's what magnifying-glass looking looks like: *It peers inside the scene to see what can be seen.*

A carpenter strikes his hammer to a nail. Head down, eyes on the target, repeatedly hitting the nail right on the head. That's what magnifying-glass looking looks like: *It concentrates on one main point.*

✳ **23** ✳

MAGNIFYING GLASS EXERCISES

Try these exercises to practice magnifying-glass looking. The first exercise aims to create a comfort level with quickly and immediately pinpointing something. The next two exercises correspond to the two approaches for spotting one main point, intentionally spotting and then instinctively spotting.

CATALOG SURFING

Find a merchandise catalog. Also secure a broad-tipped marker.

Find a comfortable seat and sit down. Flip through each page. Be sure each page is completely turned with each flip; in other words, don't flip too quickly. But do look quickly. After each flip, immediately use the marker to circle the one item on each page that grabs your attention.

(Note: Some people use sticky notes to mark certain pages when casually looking through catalogs, or they dog-ear the corner of certain pages. That's fine for denoting some pages, but in this exercise you'll want to pinpoint an item on every page.)

Continue pinpointing an item on each page until making it through the entire catalog.

Again, don't turn the pages too quickly, but do spot quickly. Immediately spot one item that stands out from all the others on each page and circle it.

Do pause, but don't pause too long. Don't think about each choice; you can always go back later, after all this magnifying-glass looking, to analyze your selections and think about the reasons you might have had to make each selection. The first time through each catalog, however, just spot and circle.

Before doing any thinking about what you picked on each page, complete one more task using magnifying-glass looking. Start flipping through the catalog again. But this time, don't point and circle something on each page; instead, spot the one item you've circled that stands out in the entire catalog. Stop when you spot it; don't feel like you have to continue through the rest of the catalog after you've spotted it. The goal is not to plow through all the pages again; the goal is to pinpoint the one overall item that stands out as the most significant.

Once you have found the significant item, take a closer look, and ask yourself: What attribute(s) of the item make it stand out? Was it something new or novel? Was it its name? Did some unusual or unique feature of the item jump out at you? Or did something else about the item strike you as iconic, capturing the spirit of the entire catalog?

REFRIGERATOR DIVING

This exercise presents magnifying-glass looking using an intentional approach.

Consider items kept in your refrigerator. Make a list in advance before beginning. Feel free to use the following list (developed with the A to XYZ method found in chapter 5) or modify it to create your list:

Applesauce	Grapes	Milk	Soda
Butter	Ham	Noodles	Turkey
Cheese	Iced tea	Orange juice	Unopened
Dip	Jam/jelly	Pickles	Vegetables
Eggs	Ketchup	Quiche	Water
Fruit	Lettuce	Roast beef	Yogurt

Once you have your list, pick one item off the list—just one. Then open the refrigerator door and see how quickly you can pinpoint that particular item. Don't scan. Spot. After spotting the item, close the door. Then pick another item off the list, open the refrigerator door, and see how quickly you can spot the item. Keep repeating (until you've worked up an appetite to eat something).

To minimize the cold air escaping from the refrigerator (increasing your electricity bill), spot the item as quickly as possible.

As an alternative to working off a list of specific items, perform the same exercise just using letters of the alphabet. Pick a letter and then dive in to pinpoint an item beginning with that letter. Repeat using different letters. Or, pick a color and perform the same exercise.

When done with the refrigerator diving, stop and ask yourself: Did you come up with any techniques, even tricks, which helped to pinpoint items quickly? Reflect on what you learned about spotting items with magnifying-glass looking.

PEOPLE SPOTTING

This exercise presents magnifying-glass looking using an instinctive approach.

Rather than spotting items from a list prepared in advance—which, as such, really aims to help practice the skill of pinpointing, and not necessarily pinpointing items of significance—for this exercise, concentrate your use of magnifying-glass looking to instinctively spot something of significance.

Prepare no list in advance. Just see how quickly you can spot something that jumps out as significant after "opening" not a literal door, but a figurative one.

Go to any one of these places frequented by a large number of people:

- Casino

- Food court at a mall

- Museum

- Public library

- Sporting event

- Trade show or conference

- Transportation (airplane, bus, or train) terminal

First, put on binoculars, find a vantage point, and scan the entire environment. Pick a specific place to station yourself and then switch to magnifying-glass looking. Now see if you can spot one person who stands out. Pinpoint a particular behavior exhibited by someone that strikes you as significant. Then imagine you were in charge of this place and ask yourself: Have you noticed anything that might suggest a way to improve the experience of the place or event?

24

SUMMARY OF
MAGNIFYING–GLASS LOOKING

W e've now taken a detailed look at three of the Six Looking Glasses. While it's very tempting to just summarize the nature of magnifying-glass looking with just a single bullet point, let's review various descriptions of encounters in the last five chapters. Each bullet point aims to enlarge our understanding of how to pause and pinpoint the one main detail of significance in any observed scene. Magnifying-glass looking

- looks closely and intensively,

- takes an extended look,

- concentrates on a single point of attention,

- looks immediately at what instinctively stands out, or, intentionally picks a criterion to pick something out,

- spots a focal point to examine,

- examines what is new or novel, notes names, locates the nucleus, or attends to the non-essential,

- notices what is most noticeable,

- locates the essence of the scene,

- looks inside the scene to see what can be seen, and

- finds the significance in what's seen.

Magnifying-glass looking is often used after scanning with binoculars or after comparing and contrasting with bifocals. It's used whenever you sense something unusual or unique about the circumstances you're in. It finds the diamond in the rough, the circle in the square, the funnel in the mall.

Now, if I had to make one main point about magnifying-glass looking, I'd say,

It looks at this, and not all that.

MICROSCOPE LOOKING

≡ Take your time and study all the details.

≡ Explore to the left and then to the right. Go up and then go down. Check in front and then in back. Peek inside and outside. Look at it every which way you can.

≡ We need to examine every single little aspect of the device.

≡ Scrutinize every behavior and really see who is trying to hide their feelings.

Have you ever watched a televised poker tournament? Cameras are embedded in the table, allowing you to see the cards held facedown by each player. Poker lingo is tossed around by TV commentators explaining the action. It is fascinating, at least until the novelty of it all wears off. These poker shows—coupled with the availability of various poker websites—have contributed greatly to the enormous popularity that this card game has enjoyed in recent years.

Join a game, and you'll quickly discover that success is not a matter of "being lucky." Successful players bring considerable skills to the table. They certainly have intimate knowledge of the various odds for different hands. They also notice numerous nuanced behaviors on the part of other players, such as facial expressions, nervous twitches, and other body language. These "tells" increase their odds of guessing what kind of cards the other players hold. Such signs can be detected from various physical behaviors, especially subtle pattern changes in eye movement (stares, glances), eyebrow movement, lip movement (bites, licks, twists), breathing (sighs, grunts), sitting adjustments (back, forward, or to the side), hand and finger positioning, chip-stacking practices, card-holding techniques, timing of bet placement, feigned attitudes, and myriad other details.

The very best players, those pros who consistently win tournaments, are highly skilled in such microscope looking. They scrutinize competitors, studying the scene, detail after detail, looking all around.

⁂ 25 ⁂

LOOKING AROUND:
SCRUTINIZING AND STUDYING

The last time I balanced my checkbook I was off by ten dollars. So I did what many of us would do: I checked my ledger entries, making sure all my additions and subtractions were correct. I was still off by ten dollars. I then double-checked the math on each entry, and still, I was off by the same amount. I then got out a pencil and marked off each deposit and check that was posted on that month's statement and made a corresponding mark in my checkbook. I remained ten dollars off. I repeated the whole process again, this time using a calculator. After all this calculating (a form of mathematical thinking) and checking (reacting to the discrepancy), it was time for just looking. I tried to spot the error (magnifying-glass looking), but nothing popped out at me. So a more thorough examination was needed. Yes, it was time for some microscope looking.

So I laid out the bank statement alongside my ledger and looked down and up the "Balance" column. I looked left to the "Amount of Payment or Withdrawal" column in my ledger, and then to the right, over to the "Checks Deducted" list on the bank statement. Nothing registered as an error. I then looked left and right again, looking more closely—checking each digit in each figure, one after another. And there it was: Check #2269, for my car payment. I had entered $334.39, the monthly lease amount, but inadvertently wrote the actual check out for $344.39. Only by scrutinizing and studying—making a full accounting of my accounting, right down to a digit by digit examination—did I find the error.

Some people would not have bothered to do all this investigation. Some might have made a $10 "adjustment" entry in their ledger. Others might have simply said to themselves, "Close enough," and lived with the discrepancy.

But close enough is not enough when doing microscope looking. With microscope looking, you seek to look closer and closer, looking around for more and more relevant details.

Think about the two motions involved in the use of an actual microscope: (1) moving the glass slide left and right, up and down—looking around at all the details, and (2) twisting the knob to adjust the power of the lens—looking more intensely at these details . Two aspects are similarly involved in microscope looking: (1) scrutinizing—by looking left and right, up and down, all around for various details, and (2) studying these details in more powerful detail.

Microscope looking requires thorough looking, taking the time to look at each and every component of what is encountered. In this way, microscope looking most differs from magnifying-glass looking. Sure, both magnifying-glass looking and microscope looking occur at a more detailed level than binoculars looking or bifocals looking. Both enlarge the view, looking more closely than the distant view taken with binoculars or the contrasting views taken with bifocals. But where magnifying-glass looking seeks to immediately spot one main detail, microscope looking seeks to more thoroughly examine additional details.

Think of it this way: If binoculars looking and magnifying-glass looking had a baby, the offspring would be microscope looking! Microscope looking very much feels like the surveying and scanning of binoculars (with grid-pattern precision), but instead of doing such at a distance, it canvasses on a more granular basis. And microscope looking feels like the detailed looking of magnifying glasses, but instead of immediately pinpointing just one detail, it scours for more details. The discovery of one interesting detail triggers exploration for more details. For if one thing strikes a chord, what else might be nearby of interest?

Microscope looking involves a more scrutinized examination and a more studied inspection than entailed with magnifying-glass looking. It takes a deep dive into the details of any particular scene. It looks for the various intricacies present in the scene, the relationships between different elements of the situation, and any contingencies and dependencies that might be present. It does not just seek to spot just one thing that is readily apparent. No, microscope looking seeks to find whatever is not obvious, whatever cannot be readily seen without taking time to uncover it.

A friend of mine has had various skin issues over the years. He has had some dermatologists completely miss (i.e., not see!) certain skin abnormalities, only to be later discovered by another physician. This friend has shared that he has had so many examinations, by so many different doctors, that he can now readily sense when a dermatologist is a really good one. He can actually feel the doctor's thoroughness, not via any physical touch, but by sensing the gaze of his examiner, intuiting the time taken to shift attention from one area of his skin to another. As the patient, he actually feels the microscope looking, as the dermatologist (at least the better ones) so closely scrutinizes and studies his condition. Thus we have the idiom of someone or something being "put under a microscope."

So why the need for microscope looking? Because we often think we have seen all there is to see when in fact there is more there than what we see. Renowned behavioral economist Daniel Kahneman has pointed out that we too often make poor decisions based on thinking "WYSIATI," What You See Is All There Is. We take action based on limited knowledge derived from what we have already seen, having neglected to see many other aspects pertinent to the situation.

Microscope looking puts what has already been seen under a microscope. Because "TIAMTBS," There Is Always More To Be Seen.

Let's now put microscope looking itself under a microscope. Let's scrutinize and study different dimensions of its use:

+ Microscope looking strives to ignore nothing.

+ Microscope looking considers everything as potentially interesting or relevant.

+ Microscope looking does not neglect anything in its study.

+ Microscope looking finds something to further scrutinize.

Microscope looking asks: What else is here? It explores. Examines. Searches. Cross-examines. Pivots. Penetrates. Plunges. It peers into, pours over, and digs into. It makes a close study. Point by point, step by step. It does not skip or scan. It rechecks, retraces, and reexamines.

With magnifying-glass looking a factory worker might find one loose bolt along the line (causing boxes to jam in one spot). With microscope looking, this worker would then go on to check all the other bolts as well as other surrounding fixtures and components of the machinery (to avoid additional jams at other spots).

✳ 26 ✳

CHECKING FOR MORE DETAILS

O f course you can become easily exhausted from excessive microscope looking. It can simply become too intense. But microscope looking need not examine "each and every detail"—in an absolute sense—in each and every circumstance. The key is to take time to look for more details, not necessarily all details. Microscope looking simply notices what would not normally be noticed without it. There may be some situations in which the microscope looking continues until you find a specific noteworthy detail (such as finding the error in an unbalanced checkbook). Or you could simply stop (or take a break) when you can no longer maintain the sustained attention.

There are some circumstances, however, that require a completely exhaustive examination. Consider a pilot and copilot performing their preflight inspection of the plane's controls and operating systems. As passengers, we want all the details scrutinized and studied via in-depth microscope looking (and not with a cursory scan). Of course, pilots work off a checklist to examine these details. But consider this: Any comprehensive checklist is the result of someone doing prior microscope looking. The very purpose of any checklist is to codify microscope looking. (For example, if I had a checklist for paying bills I probably would have caught my ten-dollar mistake before it occurred.)

Most observations, however, are not made via checklists. At any given moment, you may be called upon to examine the details of a particular situation. Such times seldom afford the luxury of moving through items on a predetermined checklist. Without such a list, you must discover what items ought to be explored in greater detail. In most circumstances, no one could have anticipated the looking required for the particular moment. The looking becomes the checking, and the checking is the in-the-moment uncovering of discoveries made while looking.

Microscope looking is looking with a "fine tooth comb." It doesn't look at the big picture, the overall scene (in which most details, by definition, are not seen). It looks at one little picture after another little picture after another—seeing what cannot be seen without such granular gazing.

Recall the scene from the classic film *E.T. the Extraterrestrial* when E.T. hid in the closet among all the plush-toy creatures. Elliott's mother opens the door and sees a closet full of stuffed animals—the "big picture." Had she done some microscope looking—scrutinizing and studying each creature one by one—she would have noticed the one poker-faced alien unlike the others. As viewers of the movie, we see E.T., because film producer Steven Spielberg has the camera slowly pan across the closet contents. This panning serves as a form of microscope looking for his audience. Spielberg's camera becomes our microscopic lens. Had the camera not panned as it did, viewers would likely have missed seeing E.T., too.

Microscope looking often uncovers that which was not spotted using magnifying-glass looking. What magnifying-glass looking cannot pinpoint, microscope looking may find when it pans for more details.

You can use microscope looking after magnifying-glass looking, especially if the magnifying glass fails to spot something significant. Similarly, microscope looking may be useful after using binoculars or bifocals looking—after something noteworthy has been identified—to look for what else might be found of note.

Skillful microscope looking really is a matter of how you go about looking for more details. The key ingredient is looking at the edges of what you see. You've heard it said, "The devil is in the details." True enough. But how then do you go about seeing these details? By looking at the edges—where one detail ends and another begins. Being fixated on one specific detail actually inhibits seeing other adjoining details. To overcome this tendency, look for the edges defining various details as a stepping stone to seeing the next one. (Interestingly, this is true biologically as well as metaphorically. For example, the retina actually works to visually enhance the edges of what's seen to sharpen the view of what is actually there.) Or look for the edges within any object of attention.

Edges represent transitions from one material, space, or time-interval to another. Find an edge and you'll find another detail. That said, let's make our own transition, as this chapter is edged out by the next.

✳ 27 ✳

SHIFTING THE OBJECT

S ometimes certain details are not seen because the edge separating one dimension of a scene from another is not readily apparent. There are hard edges and soft edges—basically, different degrees to which an edge can be identified. Some edges are so soft that one detail blurs into another. Or one detail may cover up another. Or one detail may look so similar to another that while the two are in fact distinct components, just how one differs from the other is not clear.

There is a very useful method, unique to microscope looking, which can aid in differentiating one detail from another. The method involves shifting the object. It simply involves manipulating the various items being examined—using your hands to move pieces around, alter how things touch each other, or rearrange the parts—to see detail after detail in a new or fresh way.

Think of the effort required to put together a jigsaw puzzle. At some point, after the outside edges have all been assembled to create the outer frame, after joining obvious pieces together, after making some progress with more difficult pieces, you inevitably get stuck. Perhaps only one or two pieces are needed to complete a certain section—and they're just not to be found after trying to spot them with magnifying-glass looking. When this happens, the best thing to do is to start moving the unused pieces around. You can separate them in different ways based on color, distinguishing marks, the number and position and type of tabs and pockets, and so forth. Only by shifting the pieces, touching them and rearranging them as an integral part of the looking, can you make progress in seeing the next series of pieces that fit together.

Shifting the object of looking is often fundamental to microscope looking. Different items (details in the scene) need to be nudged or shoved, stirred or rotated, pushed together or pulled apart, raised or lowered, or otherwise rearranged, to reveal more details.

When playing hide-and-seek, for example, sometimes a drape or bedspread needs to be moved to find a person who is hiding behind a curtain or a bed. When you try to find something in a purse, you often need to push items to one side or the other (or remove them altogether) to find what you are looking for. Or most basically, to see a car's engine, you have to pop the hood. You have to open any door to see what's behind it.

Watch the television show *American Pickers* and you'll see microscope looking—and its coadunate shifting of objects—at its finest. (It's purse-diving taken to a whole other level!) Stars Mike Wolfe and Frank Fritz scour the contents hoarded in old sheds, barns, garages, and other storage buildings in search of antique treasures (classic motorcycles, vintage signs, old toys, one-of-a-kind folk-art pieces, etc.). More often than not, the two must physically peel back layers and layers of amassed wares in order to see what's actually there. In fact, they pride themselves in the dirty work of rummaging through all the stuff, shifting and looking, shifting and looking, as they sift through all the clutter to find the buried riches.

The use of microscope looking need not be limited to circumstances in which all the details of a situation are unorganized and cluttered. Even in places where everything is neatly organized, it may be worth the extra effort to do some microscope looking. Most clothing stores make it a point to keep all the merchandise highly organized—neatly folded in stacks or carefully arranged by size on the rack. My wife Beth has taught me this: When shopping for clothes, don't stop looking after you've found some article of clothing you like that is the right style, color, and size. After you've found "it," keep looking. Whether it's a shirt, sweater, pair of pants, whatever kind of garment, only with continued microscope looking will you discover bad buttons, loose threads, or a faulty stitch before taking the article home. Say it's a shirt you're buying. Unfold each shirt. Check all the buttons, all the stitches, all the threads, all the seams. Grab the next one, and do the same physical checking. Grab another and another to scrutinize. Then pick the best one identified from doing the microscope looking.

Surely you've heard someone question, "How could I have missed that?" The simple answer is that someone didn't do the necessary microscope looking.

28

WHAT DOES MICROSCOPE LOOKING LOOK LIKE?

U nlike binoculars looking, which scans at a distance, microscope looking is up-close looking. Unlike bifocals looking, which pairs two opposite features, and magnifying-glass looking, which spots one significant
detail, microscope looking seeks to scrutinize multiple details. As a result,
microscope looking can often take more time to perform than the other
looking glasses.

Following are some examples of the sustained attention involved with
microscope looking:

A bank teller assists customers with deposits. When someone presents
cash in larger notes—$50 and $100 bills—the teller examines the bills to
see if they might be counterfeit. The bills are held up to the light to inspect
every detail, moving the bill ever so slowly, left and right, up and down,
to check different attributes. The portraits of Ulysses S. Grant or Benja-
min Franklin are studied to make sure no feature is too flat or muted. The
perimeter of the seal is traced to check for any uneven points. The border
is scrutinized to catch any feature that might appear blurred, even to the
slightest degree. Then the serial number is checked, one digit at a time,
between successive digits, to make sure all the numbers are evenly spaced.
Rather than using the quick stroke of a "counterfeit detection" pen (faster
for sure, but not a foolproof method to identify fakes), the worker instead
makes an effort to study the bill up close. That's what microscope looking
looks like: *It takes its time to scrutinize every detail.*

An inspector at a car fleet management company has the responsibility to check returning cars for damages. Using a form that diagrams all the areas to be examined, the fenders, bumpers, left and right doors, the hood, trunk and roof, the windows, the wheels and rims, the interior mirrors, and the seats and controls are all checked. Within each area, every square foot is scrutinized, and within each square foot, every square inch. That's what microscope looking looks like: *It examines details up and down and all around.*

A soldier, anticipating an evening inspection in the barracks, works diligently to put all gear in order and to straighten the bunk. Seeing nothing out of place, the soldier feels confident everything is in order. But then squatting down for a closer view, a paper wrapper is noticed beside the bed. After picking it up, the soldier gets on his hands and knees, looks around even more closely, everywhere around the bed, to see if there is any more trash. That's what microscope looking looks like: *Seeing one detail triggers a search for more details.*

Steelcase's collaborative workspace business, called Workspring, offers meeting rooms to its members and their guests. Each room is equipped with whiteboards and flipchart paper. To ensure no meeting participant ever experiences a faulty marker, the staff examines each and every dry-erase and flipchart marker at the end of each day. They uncap each marker and test each one on the board or paper to see if any have gone dry. Those that have dried up are thrown away. That's what microscope looking looks like: *It touches and manipulates objects to uncover and discover.*

Police detectives arrive at a crime scene. They rope off the area to carefully identify every piece of possible evidence. They make one pass, then another, and yet another, looking for more and more details. That's what microscope looking looks like: *It studies and restudies the scene.*

A young moviemaker named Spike Lee aspires to one day make great films. So he invests hours and hours watching and rewatching hundreds of movies, concentrating on the classics produced by the greatest directors of all time. But then he watches with a twist: He views the films with the sound turned off, to study each and every edit that would otherwise be obscured by the dialogue and soundtrack. Edit after edit, he studies the nature of each transition. That's what microscope looking looks like: *It examines the edges in order to see the details that usually escape notice.*

✳ 29 ✳

MICROSCOPE EXERCISES

To practice microscope looking in these exercises, you'll not only be asked to use your eyes, in some cases you'll also be asked to simultaneously use your hands. This use of hands is a very important part of the looking (by shifting or manipulating various objects). In other cases, such handiwork will precede or follow the looking, serving to call attention to the value of the microscope looking.

CHARACTER DRAWING

The nineteenth-century naturalist Louis Agassiz famously quipped, "a pencil is one of the best eyes." (He made the comment when one of his biology students, after a very thorough examination of a preserved fish, discovered it had no eyelids only after drawing the fish!) This exercise lets you experience this fact.

To do this exercise you will need to gather some drawing paper and a box of colored drawing pencils (or even a single pencil, if you like).

Select a character from the list who is most familiar to you:

- SpongeBob (from the animated TV series *SpongeBob SquarePants*)

- Red Bird (from mobile app game *Angry Birds*)

- Chuck E. Cheese (from Chuck E. Cheese's restaurant)

- Mario (from the video game *Mario*)

- Mr. Bill (from the TV show *Saturday Night Live*)

- Either spy (from *Mad Magazine*'s "Spy vs. Spy")

- Woody (from the movie *Toy Story*)

After making your selection, draw a picture from memory of the character (an act based on blindfold looking). Do the very best you can to depict the character and take as much time as you like, but do set some time limit.

After you finish, find an image of the character. A simple Internet search will do. Be sure to select the most detailed image you can find.

Then take out another piece of paper and draw your selected character again, but this time make constant reference to the actual image before you. Use microscope looking to examine each and every detail. As you study the details, replicate them as best you can with your drawing and set a more generous time limit (than for the first drawing).

As you're drawing, look from one detail to another. See how the different details relate to each other. Even look at the edges of each character feature.

When you finish your second drawing, compare the two. Notice the differences between them. Now return to microscope looking and (a) look at the details you captured in the second version, and (b) consider how you scrutinized the image to make your more detailed version. Then ask yourself: How did the microscope looking aid your drawing? Moreover: What did you find useful in looking at detail after detail?

If doing this exercise in a group, or facilitating the exercise with others, consider having actual 3-D models of these characters on-hand (most are available for sale from some source) and use these in lieu of 2-D images found online. And feel free to substitute different characters to create your own list. (E.T., anyone?)

THREE THINGS CHANGING

Find a partner for this exercise. (If done with a group, have people pair up.) Stand and face each other, and then take one minute to use microscope looking to examine what each other is wearing—moving left to right, head to toe. Afterward, turn around and face away from each other. While facing away from each other, do further microscope looking for one minute, this time to examine your own attire. Use this head-to-toe looking to identify three articles worn that could be changed, and then proceed to change these three things (e.g., unlace a shoe, switch which wrist a watch is on, loosen a belt). After changing three things, turn around to face each other again. Now do microscope looking, seeking to find the three things that were changed by the other person.

Using microscope looking, try to identify the three items that were changed on the other person. Study the other person's attire from head to toe, looking at each and every detail.

If you cannot find the three changed things by the other person, do further microscopes study, moving in the other direction, from toe to head. And if necessary, again scrutinize from left to right (and right to left) until you identify the three changes.

After each person identifies three things, repeat the microscope exercise: Turn around and choose three more items to change. Then turn around and find the three wardrobe changes on the other person.

Repeat the exercise at least five total times, in each round trying to make subtler and yet subtler changes. Be sure to keep performing microscope looking. That is, practice the serious studying and scrutinizing required of microscope looking even as the action grows more challenging.

When you finish, ask yourself: What did I have to do to sustain such microscope looking round after round?

BACKWARD PROOFING

Following is a version of a popular drill called the F-test. Read this italicized sentence and count the number of Fs:

Finished files are the result of years of scientific study combined with the experience of years.

Now do microscope looking at the same sentence, going backward starting with "s-r-a-e-y." Don't read it one word at a time; use microscope looking to examine each letter one at a time. Do you see any Fs that you missed the first time reading? (Most people miss one, two, or three of them.)

Let's get more practical: No matter how often you proofread a piece of typed writing, it always seems that some typographical error manages to sneak through. One way to catch an otherwise missed typo is to stop read-ing forward and instead look backward, one word at a time. Try it the next time you have to review some new first draft material.

Whether after doing this F-test exercise or your own backward proof-ing, ask yourself: What other situations might call four such microscope looking? (They're often right under your nose!)

SUMMARY OF
MICROSCOPE LOOKING

The use of the Six Looking Glasses method involves switching from one viewfinder to another for different kinds of observing. When it comes to microscope looking, the looking similarly switches—not from one looking glass to another, but from one detail to another, using the same lens. It involves a sustained looking at the multiplicity of details within a scene.

Let's recap some details. Microscope looking operates by

- searching and again searching,

- examining and reexamining,

- checking detail after detail,

- noticing every nuance,

- looking left, right, up, down, and all around,

- thoroughly studying in greater detail,

- looking closer and closer,

- using a fine-tooth comb,

- inspecting relationships, contingencies, and dependencies,

- exploring the edges between and within each detail,

- using your hands, manipulating the object to uncover more details, and

- always exploring what else is there to be noticed.

This type of looking puts the object of attention under a metaphorical microscope. Here it's useful to picture yourself head down, gripping the instrument with both hands, adjusting the intensity of the gaze, and shifting the object to get different detailed looks.

You seldom begin with microscope looking. Microscope looking often follows looking with other looking glasses. The results of which can trigger looping back to use other looking glasses again.

ROSE-COLORED-GLASSES LOOKING

≡ Forget the flaws. Envision how it would look if the concept were tweaked a bit.

≡ With the right modifications, this is something we could definitely emulate.

≡ I don't like the execution, but look at the way they tried to do it here.

≡ He's not much to look at now, but he has great potential.

Tony Lucadello was baseball's greatest scout, having signed fifty-two youngsters (including Hall of Famers Ferguson Jenkins and Mike Schmidt) who would rise through the minor league ranks and eventually play Major League Baseball. This number of signees making it to "the big leagues" is an order of magnitude higher than any other scout. Amazingly, Lucadello's success came despite the fact that he covered the territory of Ohio, Indiana, and Michigan, not exactly the haven of California, Florida, or Texas where the weather allows for year-round play—with better players and more opportunities to observe them.

Lucadello's scouting exploits have been chronicled by Mark Winegardner in *Prophet of the Sandlots*. Winegardner spent several summers observing Lucadello, a loveable curmudgeon who not only spurned the typical tools of his trade, the radar gun and stopwatch, but also roamed the perimeter of baseball fields instead of sitting behind home plate like most other scouts.

So how did he do it? According to Lucadello, there are four kinds of scouts: Five percent are poor scouts (who seldom plan), five percent are pickers (who just spot weaknesses), eighty-five percent are performance scouts (who look solely based on how players do—against amateur competition), but Lucadello was that rare breed of projector scout. He looked for how coachable a kid was, how a hitch in a swing or a throwing quirk might be corrected. He saw years "down the road" to envision, under the tutelage of better coaching and against stiffer competition, how a player would play. He used rose-colored-glasses looking to see the potential in talent, rather than just the current-state talent.

31

LOOKING PAST:
ENHANCING AND ENRICHING

Usually when referring to seeing the world through rose-colored glasses, the term is used to describe someone overly optimistic about things, who has a too-favorable disposition toward various affairs, who might even be in outright denial about reality. Get past that. In understanding the use of rose-colored glasses we need to have, fittingly (and ironically) enough, a more favorable view of the notion. Looking with rose-colored glasses is not utopian, but utilitarian. It's not having an unreal hope, but rather it is seeing a ray of hope in otherwise dismal circumstances. Looking with rose-colored glasses sees the promise present in any situation. It's enriching the scene by enhancing what's seen.

Simply put, rose-colored glasses look at something better than it actually is. Seeing with rose-colored glasses is not jaded looking, but it certainly is tinted looking at the objects being observed. Rose-colored glasses act in this sense like sunglasses. We wear sunglasses to filter the glare. When the sun is too bright, our vision is enhanced by wearing them.

So why don't we refer to this form of looking as sunglasses looking? For this reason: The functionality of sunglasses is insufficient to fully express what we are striving to do with this particular type of looking. With rose-colored glasses, the goal is to not only filter out but also to filter in.

Two looking functions exist as a result of using rose-colored glasses: (1) to expunge, or remove the emphasis placed on some dimension of the scene that typically or readily dominates what's seen, and (2) to exhume, or bring to light, other dimensions of the scene that might not otherwise be noticed or fully appreciated. With the use of rose-colored glasses, we take the attention off that which tends to wash out the view of everything else, so we can see something else anew.

Some consultant friends were working on a project for a small regional restaurant chain. They were charged with assessing how various elements of the place ought to be redesigned. I happened to be visiting a town that had one of this chain's restaurants. Having never been to one before, I volunteered to dine there and share my impressions afterward. Once there, I could see why my friends had been retained to do this work, for the place was riddled with shortcomings. But I donned rose-colored glasses while I ate. When it came time to provide my feedback, I prefaced my remarks by saying, "They had the right idea."

It's with the use of rose-colored glasses that you can say, "They had the right idea." Looking with rose-colored glasses sees past inadequate planning and design or past poor execution (of adequate plans and designs) to see the potential that exists in any particular situation. It's a kind of looking that looks right past what doesn't work to see what might work (if done differently).

The use of rose-colored glasses is not wishful thinking or naïve acting. To the contrary, it's a certain kind of disciplined looking that sees the potential that is there. A rose-colored view of things does not look "as if" something was or was not present. Instead, rose-colored glasses look very realistically at what actually is present. But with this lens you also look past how something has been done (ill preparedly, improperly, or poorly) to just see what has been done and why it was done (or to see what was lacking and why).

With rose-colored glasses, you peer under the surface of the scene to see the underlying structure. This type of looking sees the path and not the footprints, the general flow and not the occasional ebbs.

Where a normal glance sees current pitfalls, looking with rose-colored glasses sees future potential. It looks at lemons and sees pink lemonade!

Because of the bias we generally have against the term rose-colored, this kind of looking may strike you as irrational, a kind of looking reserved for living in fantasylands. But using this admittedly optimistic looking glass is grounded in reason: We can learn much from examining failures.

Henry Petroski, longtime professor of engineering at Duke University and a prolific writer on the subject of design, put it this way, "Form follows failure." Petroski argued against the conventional wisdom that "form follows function." So how are new functions discovered? By seeing past current failures and then seeing instead what can be done as an improvement.

To illustrate this, Petroski traces the entire history of silverware and the resulting assortment of eating utensils that exists today. He presents the evolution of utensils as an ever-evolving series of modifications based on what can only be described as rose-colored looking. Here's a recap: Once upon a time there was no silverware. A hunter uses a knife to jab a piece of meat and take it to his mouth. This works fine until one day he cuts his lip. He looks at the pointed tip and sees it rounded. The rounded knife is born. But this new knife can no longer jab pieces of food very well, so he looks at the knife and sees a fork with multiple prongs, which while pointed are too close together to cause an accidental cut. One type of fork begets another more specialized fork, and so on. Each new utensil is in essence a rose-colored version of the previous one.

The whole process of designing or redesigning any new form begins with looking at function with rose-colored glasses. It starts with seeing the defect and also seeing the opportunity to overcome that defect. Rose-colored-glasses looking does not deny the existence of flaws or defects, it just looks past them to identify the opportunity for improvement.

Rose-colored glasses can also be used to take an enhanced view of that which is already done well. When something goes as planned, we seldom look at the reasons it went well. The success factors are often taken for granted, often unexplored, and seldom formally identified. But with rose-colored glasses, even major accomplishments are seen as better than they actually are.

The whole purpose of taking a rose-colored view is to see the underlying structure below what's readily seen on the surface, beyond both the flaws and the successes.

32

FORSAKING THE FLAWS

W retched refuse. Who could see any value in wretched refuse? The tired, poor, worn out, lost, and disheveled. What good could come from such?

Consider the words from the sonnet "The New Colossus" by Emma Lazarus, engraved on a plaque at the base of the Statue of Liberty:

> Give me your tired, your poor,
> Your huddled masses yearning to breathe free,
> The wretched refuse of your teeming shore.
> Send these, the homeless, tempest-tost to me,
> I lift my lamp beside the golden door!

The United States of America was built on nothing less than the wretched refuse of the world. Where few dared to venture, Americans created a New World.

Looking with rose-colored glasses is seeing wretched refuse and welcoming it through a golden door. But it's also seeking wretched refuse to examine as something worthy of observation. Of all the looking glasses, looking with rose-colored glasses most represents a looking attitude. It advances a certain positive outlook on looking.

The purpose of rose-colored looking is to take any object normally rejected as having limited value, offering little or no possible insight, and instead seeing the untapped potential that is there to be seen. The aim is to see something as repurposed or to envision an alternative purpose. You've heard the saying, "one person's trash is someone else's treasure." To discover such treasured garbage is to have looked with rose-colored glasses.

One way to kick-start looking with rose-colored glasses is to repurpose the A to XYZ framework (introduced in chapter 5) and to use it to identify various elements you would normally be inclined to dismiss as unimportant in any particular situation. For example, let's consider the refuse that might exist in an average residential household: ashes, banana peels, old catalogs, dryer lint, ripped-open envelopes, and so forth.

Now take dryer lint. It's not much to look at, unless you don rose-colored glasses to ignore the dirty-looking, dusty-feeling nature of the material and instead see its inherent malleability. That's exactly the rose-colored virtue that two artists see in the stuff. Sandy Buffie makes lint sculptures and lint busts; Slater Barron makes similar lint sculptures but also lint portraits and lint "paintings" from not only dryer lint but also upholstery lint. Their artwork sells at handsome prices, using materials acquired at virtually no cost.

The key to using rose-colored glasses is to see the features and benefits in something instead of its flaws and blemishes. Rose-colored glasses look at anything untimely, inappropriate, unfit, and inopportune and seek to see it as something ahead of its time, appropriate for another use, fitting in different circumstances, or as an untapped opportunity to somehow be had. Instead of seeing what everything lacks, looking with rose-colored glasses recognizes that nothing is without some redeemable virtue; one just has to rosily look for it. (In this way, rose-colored looking is very green-seeking!)

Rose-colored glasses takes what is incomplete and sees it finished, what is broken and sees it fixed, what is rough-cut and sees it fine-tuned, what is unfashionable and sees it fitting in. The very nature of rose-colored-glasses looking looks at some idealized state, not just the current state.

Of course, it can be very difficult to forsake the flaws we actually see. Fortunately, there is no need to completely ignore the flaws. In fact, flaws need to be recognized when using rose-colored glasses. The trick is to see an enhanced version of any defect. To this end, it is useful to recognize that deficiencies tend to fall into two categories:

1. Acts of commission—items overtly and actively present

2. Acts of omission—items unwittingly and passively absent

With rose-colored glasses, strive to see the hidden potential in something. To do so will set you apart from those who would look at the same thing as you, only to say, "I don't see it."

33

FORESEEING OPPORTUNITIES

With rose-colored glasses the looking does not fix its gaze on noticeable flaws. This begs the question of where then to direct attention. Sure, you want to see the potential in what's seen. But how exactly do you accomplish this? Surely there must be some way to help steer your attention past obvious mistakes to instead see potential opportunities.

A checklist might help. After noticing a defect or flaw, look to opportunistically identify any of the following instead:

The underlying approach: Sometimes what stands out is the poorly performed execution of some concept. In such cases, look instead for the general approach that was taken. Was the basic plan a good one, but the merit of the method lost amid poor implementation? Instead, try seeing the same approach done correctly, not poorly.

To illustrate, consider this example: A high school basketball team stretches before practice. But every stretch is done too briefly, neglecting to hold each pose for a sufficient duration of time to do any real good. With rose-colored glasses, a coach sees the team's ability to benefit by seeing the captain count aloud to twenty for each exercise.

The overall effort: Sometimes an earnest attempt is made to do something right but fails for any number of planning and/or execution reasons. Therefore, look instead for the reasons the effort was made. Perhaps the motivation behind the flawed attempt just needs to be rechanneled. Look at the effort, not the errors.

Back to the basketball team: With rose-colored glasses, the coach might see that the team diligently performs all the stretching exercises in practice but halfheartedly does them before games. A coach wearing rose-colored glasses sees a reduced number of exercises for the team's pregame routine, so each can be done with full effort.

The basic intent: Sometimes a lack of effort may accompany poor planning and execution. Here, look instead for what triggered the whole endeavor in the first place. Can you see the real purpose behind the action? See the intent, even when it's easy to lose sight of it.

Back to our team: Yes, stretching is done to prevent injuries. But that concern can and should be addressed via individual exercises performed immediately before going into the game. The main intent of the team drills is to build team cohesion. With rose-colored glasses, a coach sees all the coaching staff joining the team for the concluding moments of the pregame drills to make sure the final exercise is done with total team unity.

The one main organizing principle: Sometimes what's observed may be so incoherent or confused, or on the other hand so straightforward and ordinary, that the intent is hard to detect. In such a case, looking with rose-colored glasses can help to see some bigger organizing principle. When looking with rose-colored glasses, don't look at specific outcomes, instead locate the organizing principle that would be there regardless of outward appearances or results.

Again, with the team example: We're looking at team exercises. With rose-colored glasses, an opportunistic coach may see the stretching as part of a grander team motivational scheme. Therefore various bench players are put in charge of different drills in an effort to keep them mentally involved even before the game begins.

The uniqueness: When all else fails, strive to see some uniqueness in the situation. When something goes uniquely awry, look at the uniqueness of the miss and not that it was amiss.

One last team example: If the team never seems to do an exercise completely in unison—say the underclassmen are always a half-step behind—a coach donning rose-colored glasses sees intentionally being off-beat as a benefit to the stretching time—to get the team loose mentally and not just physically.

Most all of this chapter has focused on five ways to look past flaws to find some hidden potential. And it used one overly drawn-out sports example to illustrate each way. Perhaps you found certain aspects of the extended illustration to be lacking. Rather than dismiss my effort, let me ask you to put on rose-colored glasses! Go back and look at each incremental point better than it actually is. Seek to see some value in its approach, effort, intent, organizing principle, and uniqueness.

Let's end with this: Any opportunity by definition is future-looking. The use of rose-colored glasses therefore looks to the future. It sees in order to foresee.

✳ 34 ✳

WHAT DOES ROSE-COLORED-
GLASSES LOOKING LOOK LIKE?

The use of rose-colored glasses represents a particular challenge. Its effectiveness hinges on seeing what is there, but seeing what's there in a form other than how it appears at the moment. Rose-colored looking requires an effort to see things better than they actually are. This can be difficult to do.

The difficulty emerges because of what you're likely to do when performing rose-colored looking. The temptation is to see some flaw and then think about how to correct it. But thinking about how to make something better is not the same as just seeing it as better. Why does this matter? Well, thinking about some deficiency may indeed lead to ideas to correct some problem, but it often does so while preserving the root cause of the problem in the first place. Rose-colored looking is not problem-solving; it's seeing new forms, new opportunities. Hopefully, you'll see the difference as we look at these examples of rose-colored looking:

Gallery Furniture in Houston, Texas, is one of the most successful furniture stores in the world, famous for its unusual store attractions—live monkeys, unique memorabilia collections, themed bathrooms, and the like. Owner Jim "Mattress Mack" McIngvale sometimes does this: When shoppers leave without making a purchase, he sends personnel out to the parking lot to ask why the visitors left without buying anything. Most retailers could never see doing such a thing (it's such an outrageously gutsy thing to do). But, for Mack, it works: Many people return to the store and then buy! And it's completely a function of Mack wearing rose-colored glasses and seeing those who exit not as non-buyers, but as his best prospects. That's what rose-colored looking looks like: *It takes a negative and sees it as a positive.*

HGTV airs a number of programs, such as *Fixer Upper*, *Love It or List It*, and *Property Brothers*, in which the very premise of the programming is based on rose-colored looking. Home improvement contractors visit various houses and unlock the potential hidden from the homeowners—who are unable to see past the current flaws. The contractors are able to envision what the home looks like better than it is at the moment. That's what rose-colored-glasses looking looks like: *It foresees the future by finding it in the present.*

The Marriott Marquis on Times Square in New York City made plans to renovate its giant atrium. Several contractors made pitches to a selection committee for the demolition phase of the project. The firm that won the work did so in part because it viewed the obvious intrusion on the guest experience as an opportunity to showcase a creative spirit. How did they accomplish this? By offering to play electro-industrial music syncopated to the jackhammer sounds and other noises anticipated during the destruction. That's what rose-colored looking looks like: *It sees opportunities.*

A juggler helps a friend learn the skill of three-ball juggling, demonstrating these steps: the toss (of one ball), catch (of same ball), exchange (two tosses/catches), then juggling (two exchanges). The friend follows along, step after step, failing each time—drop after bumbling drop. But the two never discuss the drops, concentrating instead on the way each step was approached, the effort made, the intent behind each step, and the "scooping" motion that precedes each toss. Suddenly, the friend make an unexplained adjustment, and voilà—Juggling! That's what rose-colored looking looks like: *Instead of fixing shortcomings, it fixates on what's coming.*

A child takes lessons to learn to play a musical instrument. The instructor doesn't catalog all the mistakes made in each class but treats each stumble as a platform to emphasize what could be done. Recitals are not used to lock in grades but are seen as occasions to unlock potential. That's what rose-colored looking looks like: *It treats each situation as a future success.*

Don't like some of the previous five examples? Well, look at them again and see only what helps illustrate the nature of rose-colored looking. For that's what rose-colored looking looks like: *It looks at something better than it actually is.*

ROSE-COLORED
GLASSES EXERCISES

Any exercise aimed at practicing rose-colored-glasses looking will tend to involve interaction with objects of attention that are generally viewed unfavorably. To practice rose-colored-glasses looking, it makes sense to look at things with few redeeming qualities—those topics we generally avoid. It's tempting, for example, to take a rose-colored look at death and taxes. Instead, we'll examine some other items and interactions, ones some of us merely find deadly and taxing.

WHITE-ELEPHANT HUNTING

Consider the category of goods called "white elephants"—items for which the negative features (ugliness, vagueness, bulkiness, and so forth) far outweigh any benefit of possessing them, and are therefore difficult to give away (i.e., no one else wants them, even for free). They often serve as gag gifts, gift-wrapped and exchanged at white-elephant parties. (By the way, the very existence of white-elephant events demonstrates that someone has donned rose-colored glasses—seeing some good found in such items, and the opportunity for the items to be exchanged for other similarly ambiguous worth.) This exercise directs rose-colored looking at such items.

Invite someone to join you for this rose-colored adventure. You'll need a team of two to do it. Decide upon a suitable venue where you might find potential white-elephant items for sale (places that represent last-ditch attempts to sell the stuff). Candidates for finding these items include flea markets, garage sales, yard sales, and estate sales. Lacking these options, try a thrift shop or even a dollar store.

Go to the selected venue with your partner. If visiting garage sales, consider making multiple stops to make a morning of it. When you get to your selected venue, the two of you will assume two different roles.

In the first role, both of you should first put on magnifying glasses to spot an item independently deemed to be of the least possible value of any item on display. In other words, find something for which its greatest significance is its insignificance!

Once you each have spotted such an item, exchange items with each other. Then in the second role, switch to rose-colored glasses and look at your newly acquired item. Look past its many flaws and instead seek to see some potential present in the item. Look at the item as better than it actually is. Seek to see some unforeseen opportunity to put the item to an alternative use. Ask yourself: How can I see this item used in a uniquely positive way?

After doing this rose-colored looking, repeat the exercise—with each person spotting and selecting another item, exchanging it, and then repeating the rose-colored looking. Do this at least three or four times.

Finally, repeat the exercise once more but skip the exchange. That is, do the rose-colored-glasses looking on your own—grabbing various items of suspect value using magnifying-glass looking and then immediately switching to rose-colored glasses to see the potential that exists in each item. One further suggestion: Find five such items, assemble them as a set, and use rose-colored glasses to see an opportunity to use them all in some new collective way.

FLYING THE ROSE-COLORED SKIES

Commercial air travel, never too convenient to begin with, has become particularly burdensome these days. No matter where you go, flying has become a major hassle. That hassle is great fodder for rose-colored looking.

So the next time you fly, treat the trip as an opportunity to don rose-colored glasses. Each step along the way, look at the process better than it actually is. Wear rose-colored glasses to see a better version of flight check-in, baggage checking, security clearance, gate seating, boarding, baggage stowage, in-flight food and beverage, deplaning, and baggage claim. (If nothing more, doing this rose-colored looking will make any inconveniences more tolerable.)

Don't look at the shortcomings as shortcomings. Don't even look at them as stepping stones to a better way. Instead, look at them as stepped-on stones. View any frustrating element of the process as an alternative new practice that might be foreseen. For example, I saw a version of TSA pre-check years before it emerged. Decades ago, I envisioned lie-flat seats. Today, with rose-colored glasses, I see early overhead-baggage boarding (bags are boarded before the passengers), talking and non-talking sections, and rear rows sponsored by Match.com.

Do your own rose-colored-glasses looking, and ask yourself: Why don't the airlines see it this way? Perhaps someone needs to hand their executives some rose-colored glasses.

MAG-AD-LIBBING

Recall in chapter 11, the exercise for practicing binoculars looking that involved the surveying of all magazines at a magazine stand. Here, a single magazine issue will suffice to practice rose-colored-glasses looking. So find a popular magazine lying around the house or workplace, preferably one with lots of advertisements.

Once you have a single magazine in hand, find a seat, sit down, and fasten your rose-colored glasses. Ready? Really? Remember, looking with rose-colored glasses requires a certain attitude.

Flip open the magazine and stop at the first ad that you encounter. (Note: You are not doing microscope looking here, so avoid searching left to right or right to left to study every ad. Just stop at the first one.) Regardless of whether you find the ad appealing or not, look at it with rose-colored glasses. Look at it better than it actually is. Don't ignore obvious weaknesses that you see. Instead, see in these weaknesses some strength in the artwork and word copy. What opportunities do you see to use the general approach, effort, intent, organizing principle, or some other uniqueness there in the ad in an enhanced way? What would an enriched version of the advertisement look like? See it that way now. Then ask yourself: What would an ideal ad, based on what you see, look like?

When you are done looking with rose-colored glasses, do the same exercise again with another randomly selected ad. If you have multiple magazines around, feel free to switch issues to locate each successive ad.

36

SUMMARY OF ROSE-COLORED- GLASSES LOOKING

Of the five looking glasses that we've examined thus far, rose-colored glasses represents the one most counter to our everyday experience. To survey and scan (with binoculars), compare and contrast (with bifocals), pause and pinpoint (with a magnifying glass), and scrutinize and study (with microscope looking), we don't necessarily need to look in completely foreign ways. These types of looking just demand that it be done more intentionally, deliberately, and formally. But with rose-colored-glasses looking, the observer must look in a way altogether different from any norm. It requires simultaneously looking at the world as it is but at the same time envisioning it better than it actually is.

Not to be negative here (view what follows as better than it actually is), but let's posit a series of "not" statements as the means to summarize this section.

Looking with rose-colored glasses

- does not pick on current weaknesses but looks at "down the road" potential;

- is not utopian, but utilitarian;

- is not an unreal hope but does look for a ray of hope;

- not only filters out the bad but also filters in the good;

- looks not if someone fell short, but if someone had "the right idea";

- is not wishful thinking or naïve thinking, but disciplined looking;

- does not just see how it's done, it also looks at what was done and why;

- does not see form following function but sees form following failure;

- does not just accept what's in view, it enhances and enriches that view;

- is not just an approach to looking, it's also an attitude of looking;

- does not dismiss anything as unimportant but sees the potential in all things; and

- does not just see the current state but envisions some idealized state.

Rose-colored-glasses looking finds an underlying approach, overall effort, basic intent, organizing principle, or any other uniqueness it foresees as the basis for the future.

BLINDFOLD LOOKING

≡ *Let's reflect on what we've seen and pick out our favorite features.*

≡ *What do you recall most about what you've observed?*

≡ *Consider all that happened and look for just the few things that matter most.*

≡ *Stop searching any further and look back at what stands out so far.*

O ver the past twenty-five years, there have been more than three-hundred post-conviction exonerations in the United States based on DNA evidence. These convictions were reversed due to DNA analysis. And many of those wrongfully charged had been found guilty based in part on eyewitness misidentification during a police lineup.

These misidentifications were not so much a function of the witnesses doing a poor job of looking at those in the lineup, which includes both the primary suspect and the "fillers" or extra individuals added to the line. Witnesses are given plenty of time to carefully scrutinize each person in line. In many cases, they even have the option to make no choice if they're at all uncertain. Instead, the problem rests in taking an inaccurate look at the image of the perpetrator in the mind of the witness. It's often an inability to see the person in the mind's eye, to look back and accurately see the past, which leads to the misidentification.

Research indicates that sequentially viewing each person in any given lineup one at a time—looking at people (or photographs) one after another—instead of all at once, seems to result in less misidentification. Why is that? Well, the witness is less likely to rely upon relative comparisons between different individuals in the lineup now, and instead compare each person to the past in their mind. Such demonstrates the nature of blindfold looking—seeing what is there while not observing it right there.

Don't think this odd. It's the very skill used by sketch artists to reliably and accurately render a drawing of a crime suspect they've never even seen.

✳ 37 ✳

LOOKING BACK:
LOOKING AT LOOKING

The National Film Board of Canada produced an animated film directed by Eva Szasz called *Cosmic Zoom*. The eight-minute animation depicts a boy and his dog in a rowboat. After the lad rows for a few seconds, the image momentarily freezes. Then the animation resumes and starts to zoom up and away from the boy. Soon, the viewer can see the outline of the Ottawa River, then the city of Ottawa, and next the surrounding countryside. As the camera continues to zoom away, all of eastern Canada comes in view, then North America, and then the entire earth. The moon shoots by, then Mars, eventually Jupiter, later Saturn, Uranus, Neptune, and Pluto. Then the whole Milky Way comes in view, followed by other galaxies, and on to the edge of the universe.

The image freezes again. Then the camera begins to zoom back down, back through the galaxies, the Milky Way, the outer planets, past the moon to Earth, North America, Canada, Ottawa, the river, and again to the boy in the boat. The view continues to zoom down, focusing on the boy's hand, upon which sits a mosquito. The camera continues its zoom, to the mosquito's proboscis. Then to the skin surface—with its hair shafts and sweat gland pores—penetrating the epidermis, the dermis, past capillaries, cell membranes, to organelles, molecules, atoms, and then subatomic particles.

The scene freezes once more.

Then the camera zooms back up through the atomic structure, molecular system, and biological tissue, returning to the boy's hand, to the mosquito, and back to the boy. Then cut: back out to the original scene of the boy and his dog in a rowboat. Another momentary freeze frame, then the action resumes with the boy once again rowing away.

The short animated film provides a wonderfully charming look at looking.

Let's take a look at the different lenses demonstrated in this film: the zooming itself is reminiscent of keeping a distance (binoculars); the zooming out and zooming in pairs opposites (bifocals); the pinpointed spot on the mosquito (magnifying glass); all the details of space and the human body (microscope looking); and the viewer never actually seeing the mosquito bite or boy swat (rose-colored glasses). All these forms of looking are on display in the production.

But the climactic moment occurs when the screen goes dark, completely black, in outer space, right before zooming back down. In that extended moment, you look back over time and space—back at what was there, is there, without any of what's there in actual view.

Consider a less cosmic, yet similarly instructive example: You can watch a hot air balloon gradually ascend—up, up, and away—until out of sight. But then you can still see it, imagine it, in your mind.

Blindfold looking is a lens for considering: What's really been seen? It's a way of "going dark," of no longer looking at any object in actual view at the moment, in order to look instead at prior looking. It's seeing something in the mind's eye. With each of the other five looking glasses, you look at what's out there, right now; with blindfolds, you recall what you saw or didn't see in the past.

Blindfold looking looks at not only what has been seen; it also looks at what has not been seen. And you also look at what might have been mistakenly seen as one thing, when in fact it was another.

There is a form of thinking described as metacognition—thinking about thinking. (Dr. de Bono calls it Blue Hat thinking as part of his Six Thinking Hats method.) Similarly, there is a form of looking that can be described as metaobservation—looking at looking. This is blindfold looking.

As such, blindfold looking is a non-cognitive skill. That is, it's not thinking about what you have remembered; rather it's just re-seeing what you saw.

Is there really a difference between seeing what you saw and thinking about what you remember? Certainly, because you see much in any moment that you cannot later remember. In fact, by putting on blindfolds and making a deliberate attempt to take another look—in the mind's eye—you can often trigger long lost memories. This relooking prompts a new thought or even recalls some old forgotten thought.

The use of blindfolds need not involve any formal visualization process, in terms of channeling some sort of meditative energy. No divination is implied. But there is a simple process involved. It involves disabling all other forms of looking aimed at the object of attention—and instead attending to the eye's attending.

Blindfold looking looks back at the past. But interestingly, this backward looking can also be used to look at the present and into the future. That sounds strange, certainly, but it can be done. Here's how:

Blindfold looking at the past: This is like a retrospective looking back "over the years," where you recall what you have seen. You simply see it again in your mind's eye. (This is admittedly the dominant use of blindfold looking.)

Blindfold looking in the present: This is akin to visual journaling, a "sense memory" technique a method actor might practice to help recall, say, the contents of a room—while in that very room. After a while the looking stops, and each item is recalled. The looking and then not-looking is repeated until what's there is readily seen in the mind's eye.

Blindfold looking into the future: To practice this, before entering some space, put on blindfolds to see what you anticipate in your mind's eye. Going beyond binoculars looking, this approach takes a view above and beyond any physical vantage point—to see what you see coming. It's a look "back to the future."

Sometimes looking in these ways will feel like a game of pin the tail on the donkey or whacking away at a piñata. You may be blindfolded, but what's there is still there, if you only look with blindfolds.

✳ 38 ✳

ASSESSING THE LOOKING

Sometimes the very act of looking gets in the way of seeing something. We become so absorbed in looking at some aspect of the viewed object—whether using binoculars, bifocals, magnifying glasses, microscopes, rose-colored glasses, or donning no particular glasses at all—that we miss other elements of the scene. We might, for example, be so intent in watching our child swinging on a swing set that we miss seeing someone else's child walking toward the swing line about to get hit. Or we're so fixated on potential safety hazards that we fail to see and enjoy the kid having fun.

We can never take in all that there is to see, certainly not all at once. Having a portfolio of looking glasses at your disposal, and using each in turn, helps you see more than you would otherwise without wearing any of them. The purpose of blindfold looking, in particular, aims to further assist this effort, to see what is missed even after using the other five looking glasses.

Logically then, blindfolds are often worn at the conclusion of some observational exploration. But like binoculars, which can be used episodically in the beginning, middle, and end of an exploration, blindfolds can be used to start, interrupt, and conclude an overall observation effort. In each instance, the blindfolds serve to impart greater objectivity and impartiality. How so? By not letting previous observations bias further observations.

Consider Lady Justice, the mythical Roman goddess so often found in statue form outside courthouses. How is she depicted? She's usually blindfolded, of course, representing the blind eye of justice. She's not blind, however. Instead, she's blinded to more clearly and objectively see what is laid before her.

Blindfold looking is not the absence of looking. It's just a different kind of looking. It is sight, exercised unlike the other forms of looking that are directed at the object of attention. The difference is it directs your attention to the act of looking. It assesses what kind of looking has taken place and how productive such looking has been. It determines what additional looking—and kind of looking—should take place. Like a "blindfolded" judge overseeing evidence in a courtroom, blindfold looking decides what should be admitted and what should be barred from being seen. It seeks to have a clear picture of all that's taken in.

Just as binoculars looking may inform an observer where to look, blindfold looking provides perspective on how to look. Of course, such blindfold looking benefits from the prior use of the other looking glasses. If the other looking glasses have been thoroughly and rigorously used, resulting in a rich mix of observation-based insights, blindfolds might be able to draw some conclusions about what has been seen. But if observations using the other looking glasses are found lacking, blindfolds take on a different role.

In this case, blindfold looking assesses how well the other looking glasses have been used. Blindfold looking then determines what additional binoculars, bifocals, magnifying glass, microscope, and rose-colored looking might be needed. Recall the sketch artist, who must judge whether a composite can be accurately determined, or whether there is "not enough to go on" without additional input. To render an accurate drawing, the sketch artist must not only look at the work in progress but also at what he is seeing in his mind. And most importantly, he must determine if additional information from the witnesses is needed.

Blindfold looking therefore looks at what has already been looked at, is stored in the mind's eye, and ready to be assessed. It seeks to then assess two main characteristics of this other looking, categorized as gems and gaps.

Gems are highly prized observations, clearly seen as offering new insights. Whereas gaps are inadequately performed observations, or altogether neglected observations, clearly pointing to the need to initiate or revisit the use of some of the other looking glasses.

One way to go about looking for gems is to look for them in three subcategories: primary gems, secondary gems, and tertiary gems. A simple three-part process of looking for gems can be employed. Look for yourself and ask: (1) What observations really stand out? (2) What else stands out? (3) And is there anything else that stands out?

To see gaps, use an even simpler process and ask: (1) What major gaps do you see? (2) What minor gaps do you see? In other words, try to see what you did not see.

39

RECALLING THE LOOKING

Your car is recalled. This can mean one of either two different things. Either your vehicle has some defect, the result of some poor quality manufacturing process. Or, you're reminiscing about an automobile you once owned. In the first case, you send the car back for repairs; in the latter case, you simply recollect certain features of the automobile that once charmed you.

These two meanings of recall represent the two manners in which blindfold looking can be employed. Let's call these Recall-What and Recall-How:

Recall-What: This is blindfold looking that assesses observations.

Recall-How: This is blindfold looking that assesses the observing.

Thus, blindfold looking recalls not only what was observed (Recall-What) but also recalls how these observations were gleaned (Recall-How). These two aspects of blindfold looking are of course related, since how you see influences what you see.

Recall-What looks at what observations resulted from the use of other looking glasses. It sees what was seen—what stood out or seemed meaningful or at least memorable.

Recall-How looks at what looking glasses were used, are being used, or are planned for use as well as how each looking glass is used. You can ask: Were any of the looking glasses used insufficiently? Were any used incorrectly? Or ineffectively?

So to recap: What was seen is Recall-What. How it was seen is Recall-How.

Recall-What also sees what was not seen. To explore this, you can ask: What was surprisingly absent from what was seen? What would you expect to recall, but seems missing? Recall-How also notices what looking glasses were not used that perhaps should have been used.

In the end, both Recall-What and Recall-How simply seek to identify looking glasses that ought to be used or reused again.

Consider the examination of dogs in a dog show. Initially, all the competing dogs are paraded around the arena. Each is examined as they pass by the judge. The judge looks at each dog's overall appearance and temperament (at a distance, with binoculars), gait when moving and stance when at rest (with bifocals), general size and shape (with magnifying glass). The field gets narrowed down to a few possible winners. Then the judge stops looking at any dog in particular, and looks instead with blindfolds—recalling what all was observed (Recall-What) and recalling how everything was observed (Recall-How). Then what's seen in the judge's eye triggers a decision to give a "second look" to certain dogs, examining (with a microscope) specific characteristics such as a dog's coat, ears, eyes, feet, tail, muscle tone, or bone structure. (If judges are honest, they will tell you they sometimes go back and don rose-colored glasses, never worn on the first pass, to see if they mistakenly thought they saw some flaw. That is, they decide when blindfolded to use rose-colored glasses to give some dogs a second chance, sometimes correcting their thinking after more detailed looking.)

The process of donning blindfolds can be done formally, in a rigorous way, recalling the use of any of the other looking glasses:

- Binoculars with Recall-What: What did you see while surveying and scanning?

- Binoculars with Recall-How: Could you find a better vantage point?

- Bifocals with Recall-What: What did you see while comparing and contrasting?

- Bifocals with Recall-How: Could you use an alternative pairing?

- Magnifying glass with Recall-What: What did you see while pausing to pinpoint?

- Magnifying glass with Recall-How: Could you spot something else as significant?

- Microscope with Recall-What: What did you see while scrutinizing and studying?

- Microscope with Recall-How: Could you explore for even more details?

- Rose-colored glasses with Recall-What: What was improved and enhanced?

- Rose-colored glasses with Recall-How: Could you foresee a different opportunity?

Blindfold looking is not passive looking. It's actually actively looking at what was seen (and not seen) with the looking glasses used (or not used) in order to direct further looking.

WHAT DOES BLINDFOLD
LOOKING LOOK LIKE?

Before we look at some examples of what blindfold looking looks like, it only seems logical to first take a moment to consider what blindfold looking does not look like: Blindfold looking does not necessarily require closing your eyes (although that might help); it does not involve entering some meditative state; it does not mean no longer looking at all; and it is not the avoidance of looking.

Indeed, blindfold looking is still looking. It looks like this:

A newspaper reporter has just returned to his desk from the scene of a natural disaster. Looking back and recalling the devastation seen, but no longer in the physical presence of the destruction, both the overall damage and the particular details about the place, the people, and the early steps of recovery underway are nevertheless seen. Sure, the reporter checks recorded notes for quotes from various citizens and first responders who were earlier interviewed. But to actually describe the site, no notes need checking. The scene is seen in the mind. The front-page story the next day vividly captures the heartbreaking sights. That's what blindfold looking looks like: *It takes a look at looking (to see what was seen).*

A bobsledder heads down a challenging course. Approaching a difficult three-turn combination, each curve is seen. Not literally, of course, since the sled travels far too quickly to maintain any prolonged glance at the track. In the moment, the bobsledder does not just look at what is "out there" but instead sees what has been seen before. The combinations of turns are viewed mentally. That's what blindfold looking looks like: *It sees what's in the mind's eye (and looks at what's "already there")*.

A small group of Las Vegas conventioneers step out for a walk at night. As they cross the bridge over Las Vegas Boulevard, they notice "The Grand Canyon Experience" on the other side. Curious to visit, they first stop to consider what they expect to see when they visit the place. They look at the outlet before actually arriving at it, anticipating what they'll see. They look in their minds to see what they might soon enjoy, learn, ride, behold— indeed experience! That's what blindfold looking looks like: *It makes metaobservations about other observations (past, present, and even future)*.

A couple takes a vacation in The Netherlands. In Amsterdam, they visit the Van Gogh Museum. Before heading out, they recall many of their favorite paintings they have seen. They also note how pleasantly surprised they were to take in a special exhibit of Paul Gauguin's works that was also on display. As they look back on the visit, they suddenly realize they have not seen *The Starry Night*, so they go back to find it. That's what blindfold looking looks like: *It recalls what was seen and what was not seen*.

That same couple, after finding *The Starry Night*, head to the gift shop. Before shopping, they look back on how they looked at the art throughout the museum. They see that they always stayed together. So in the store, they decide to split up and separately look for potential items to buy. (They also decide that for their next art museum visit, they'll spend some brief amount of time looking at the art on their own.) That's what blindfold looking looks like: *It recalls how the looking was conducted (and makes adjustments for further and future looking)*.

A wedding planner looks back at a recently arranged reception and sees how a number of new design elements were well received by the bride and groom and by their guests. A few overlooked details are also seen, despite going undetected by others at the time. That's what blindfold looking looks like: *It looks for gems and looks for gaps (and sees what others may not have noticed in what's been seen)*.

✷ 41 ✷

BLINDFOLD EXERCISES

U sing blindfolds requires especially deliberate and disciplined effort. It involves a pronounced switch from looking at the object of attention to looking at the looking itself. This change takes the eye off examining the object and puts the attention on the mind's eye, to what it has seen and how it has seen. Exercises to practice blindfold looking necessarily require some prior observation activity. So for each of these exercises you will be asked to first do some other forms of looking before donning blindfolds.

PICTURE RECALLING

Obtain a coffee-table book rich with photographs, preferably one with a single photograph on each page. Open the book up at random and select a single picture to examine. Don't worry about putting on any particular looking glass to examine the image. Take as much time as you like, looking in any way you like. Then close the book and put on your blindfolds.

First, do Recall-What and recall what you saw in the photograph. Make a list of all the characteristics—from general impression to specific elements—that you saw in the picture. Or feel free to draw a rough schematic that sketches out the relative positioning of the various features of the picture that you now observe. With the book closed, no longer looking at the actual picture, see the picture in your mind's eye, and ask yourself: What stands out in the picture you're now seeing? What was seen that you still see?

Next, do Recall-How and assess your initial looking. Consider how you went about looking at the picture. If you were to look again at another picture in the book, look at how you would look at it differently than the previous one. Then ask yourself: What other looking glasses would you choose to use? In what order would you use them?

With this completed, take off your blindfold. Return to the coffee-table book and pick a new page at random. Repeat the same process: Look over a specific picture for as long as you like (perhaps using lessons learned from the blindfold looking for the first picture). Close the book and again do Recall-What and Recall-How.

Keep repeating this routine (for as long as you like). Establish this goal for yourself as you practice blindfold looking with this exercise: With each successive page you open, spend less time looking at the selected picture. Yet try to see more of the picture in your mind during Recall-What. And with each successive turn, further refine your Recall-How looking, until you feel you have come close to perfecting your looking approach.

BLINDFOLD-AND-SEEKING

This exercise will function very much like the previous one, except in lieu of looking at pictures in a coffee-table book, different items in different rooms of your home or workplace will be examined. Pick a building in which you have already spent considerable time and are greatly familiar with the place—at least in general.

Set up a "home base," much like if you were playing a game of hide-and-go-seek. While at home base, think of an item you know is in another room. Once you have selected that item, put on your blindfold for about thirty seconds. The whole time you are blindfold looking, picture the item in your mind using Recall-What. (You'll likely have a hard time sustaining this blindfold looking for the full thirty seconds.) Look back and ask yourself: What do you recall seeing?

Once done with Recall-What, do some blindfold looking using Recall-How. Ask yourself: What looking would you want to do when you actually go see the item to help recall more about it? What looking glass would you use?

After doing this blindfold looking with Recall-What and Recall-How, go to the selected room and item. Look it over—with the looking glasses that you chose using Recall-How—and do so for as long as you like. When you finish looking at the actual item, return to home base, and repeat your blindfold looking. Count to twenty this time while you do Recall-What. Then refine your Recall-How looking.

When you finish, go see the item again. Look it over, but spend less time looking than when you made your initial visit. And when you finish, return to home base. Do Recall-What again, counting just to ten this time. (Try to see more in your mind each turn, using even less time!)

Repeat this process for another item in a different room. Keep going with different items until you are ready to do some Recall-How looking at the entire exercise.

RE-EXERCISING

For our final exercise with blindfold looking—indeed for all of the Six Looking Glasses—look back at all the previous exercises in earlier sections of this book:

- Coffee Shop Canvassing

- Monumental Snapshotting

- Magazine Rack-a-Touring

- Groceries-Pairing

- Cereal Box Flipping

- Room-inating

- Catalog Surfing

- Refrigerator Diving

- People Spotting

- Character Drawing

- Three Things Changing

- Backward Proofing

- White-Elephant Hunting

- Flying the Rose-Colored Skies

- Mag-Ad-Libbing

Do some blindfold looking, looking back on each of these exercises, one at a time. For each, first do Recall-What, asking yourself: What do you see in your mind right now from when you previously did these looking exercises?

Then feel free to glance back in the book and re-read the instructions for each exercise (in chapters 11, 17, 23, 29, and 35). Then, again, put on blindfolds and do Recall-What. Try to see what you saw before in your mind. Finally, do Recall-How and ask yourself: How would you go about looking differently if you were to repeat each exercise?

SUMMARY OF
BLINDFOLD LOOKING

Our examination of each of the Six Looking Glasses is now complete. Before moving on to study some additional approaches on how to use the full set of looking glasses, let's look back on what has been discussed concerning blindfold looking.

Recall that blindfold looking

- serves as metaobservation, looking at other looking;

- "goes dark" to see what's in the mind's eye;

- looks at what has been seen and what has not been seen;

- also looks at how one looks;

- most often looks back at past looking but can also look "in the moment" as well as look "back to the future";

- is not the avoidance of looking but is just a different kind of looking;

- directs your attention to looking itself;

- provides perspective on how to look;

- assesses how well you have looked;

- categorizes observations as gems and gaps;

+ recalls the observations: what has been seen; and

+ recalls the observing: how one has seen.

Blindfold looking can look back on looking that was done with binoculars. It can look back on looking that was done with bifocals. It also can look back on magnifying glass and microscope looking. It can even look back on rose-colored looking. And yes, it can even look back on itself, on blindfold looking!

Blindfolds help ensure the observer practices what ought to be done with each looking glass, by paying attention to the looking. Blindfolds remind you to stop, look, and listen.

LOOKING
TO
LEARN

✳ **43** ✳

EVERYDAY LOOKING

Equipped with all Six Looking Glasses, anyone can become a better observer. There certainly will be opportunities to use the Six Looking Glasses tool in deliberately planned ways (we'll get to those in the next two chapters), but the most immediate benefit of the tool comes with simply being aware of both (a) the availability of any looking glass to be donned at any time, as well as (b) the availability of your surroundings to be looked at in any moment. The easiest way to make greater and better observations is to use a single looking glass on various occasions that can arise each and every day.

Such everyday looking simply involves recognizing circumstances in which a particular looking glass might be used. To illustrate, following are some everyday circumstances that might arise for using a particular looking glass:

 Binoculars: Use when visiting some place for the first time, when entering any place, when exiting any place, when feeling crowded, or when overwhelmed with details.

Bifocals: Use when you are familiar with some place or thing, when everything seems the same (in the moment), when everything seems the same (as before), or when you are bored.

Magnifying: You can use when in a hurry, when overwhelmed with details, when overwhelmed with details and in a hurry, or when you know what you want to find but can't.

 Microscope: Use when fascinated by something, when baffled by something, when faced with some difficulty, or when there is "time to kill."

 Rose-colored: Use when all goes awry, when nothing seems positive, when some place or thing is not to your taste, or when interrupted, disturbed, or even offended.

 Blindfold: You can use when transitioning from one place to another, after completing some task, at the end of any visit, at the end of the day, or at the start of the day!

Now, we turn to ways to more deliberately use the Six Looking Glasses.

44

LOOKING ROUTINES

Some circumstances lend themselves to employing the Six Looking Glasses in a more systematic way, utilizing a particular observation routine. Any such routine represents a specific prearranged order in which the different looking glasses are used, one after another.

Following is a portfolio of a dozen such looking routines to use in various general situations. No absolute right or wrong order is suggested in outlining these routines. Each just represents a starting point for structuring routines to make certain observations. Start out trying them as outlined. Feel free over time to modify any of these routines based on your actual experience.

LOOKING ROUTINES
Finding a Lost Item:

 Blindfold: Look back at where you have recently been with the item. (Then go to each place, one at a time.)

 Magnifying: Try to immediately spot the item.

Rose-colored: Look where it would ideally be.

Bifocals: Look in logical places; then look in opposing places.

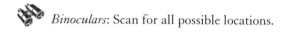 *Binoculars*: Scan for all possible locations.

 Microscope: Look in detail in each possible location.

Repeat as necessary; stop whenever and wherever the item is found.

Entering and/or Exiting any Place:

 Blindfold: Consider what you expect to see as you enter/exit.

 Microscope: Examine details as you enter/exit.

 Magnifying: Spot one main detail to look at more closely.

Blindfold: After entering/exiting, look back and consider what you saw.

Exploring a New Environment:

 Binoculars: Find a vantage point and from there survey the overall scene.

 Magnifying: Spot something to look at in greater detail.

 Microscope: Look nearby for other details in the surrounding area.

Then treat wherever you are as a new vantage point and repeat.

Revisiting a Familiar Environment:

 Binoculars: Find a vantage point and from there scan for anything unusual.

 Magnifying: Spot something out of the ordinary to look at up close.

Rose-colored: Look at that same item better than it actually is.

Then treat wherever you are as a new vantage point and repeat.

Conducting an Inspection:

 Magnifying: Pick one item or feature and closely examine it.

Bifocals: Look at that same object in some opposing way.

 Microscope: Look closer for more details.

Binoculars: Step back and scan for anything you might have missed.

Microscope: Look closer for more details.

Pick another item or feature and repeat.
After exhausting every possibility:

 Blindfold: Look back and consider what was seen and not seen.

Seeking a Discovery:

Magnifying: Spot something to examine closely.

Rose-colored: Look at that object better than it actually is.

Magnifying: Reexamine that same object closely.

Bifocals: Look at that object in some opposing way.

Rose-colored: Look at that opposing way better than it actually is.

Repeat as desired.

Investigating a Problem:

Magnifying: Try to immediately spot the cause of the problem.

Bifocals: Look for a polar opposite cause.

 Blindfold: Consider where you have not looked.

 Magnifying: Try to immediately spot the cause of the problem.

 Microscope: Closely look nearby for other possible causes.

 Blindfold: Consider where you have not looked.

Repeat as necessary.

Examining a Physical Item:

 Binoculars: Stand back from the item and survey it from a distance.

 Rose-colored: Look at the item better than it actually is.

 Magnifying: Spot the one main feature.

 Bifocals: Look at this feature in some opposing way.

 Microscope: Manipulate the item, looking at every detail.

 Blindfold: Consider what feature(s) strike you as most significant.

Deciphering a Process:

 Binoculars: Find a vantage point and scan the process from a distance.

 Magnifying: Pinpoint the step that looks most critical.

 Microscope: Examine every step in detail from beginning to end.

 Rose-colored: Look at the process better than it actually is.

 Bifocals: Examine every step, from end to beginning.

 Magnifying: Pinpoint the step that looks most critical.

Rose-colored: Look at the process better than it actually is.

Witnessing an Event:

 Binoculars: Find a vantage point and survey the event from a distance.

Magnifying: Spot an activity that looks most compelling.

Bifocals: Look at that activity in some opposing way.

Magnifying: Spot an activity that looks the least compelling.

Rose-colored: Look at that activity better than it actually is.

Find a new vantage point and repeat.

Taking a Tour:

 Binoculars: At each tour stop, locate a vantage point.

Magnifying: Spot some detail at each stop that stands out.

Bifocals: Look for some opposing dimension to that detail.

 Microscope: As time permits, look around for additional details.

Blindfold: Between stops, look back on what you just saw.

Waiting in Line:

 Binoculars: Treat your spot in line as a vantage point to scan the scene.

Magnifying: Spot something or someone that stands out.

Microscope: Examine this thing or person in greater detail for more details.

When the line moves, treat your new position as a new vantage point and repeat.

The main purpose in outlining these general routines is to demonstrate how the looking glasses can be used in different combinations in different circumstances. Notice that a given looking glass may be used more than once in a particular routine; also note that not all looking glasses are necessarily used in every routine.

There are also many specific circumstances where you can use some routine. Every conceivable circumstance of course cannot be addressed here. But to illustrate such looking routines, here are six looking routines for six different specific situations.

Home Buyer Checking Out a Potential New House:

 Binoculars: Find a vantage point outside to check the house's "curb appeal."

Magnifying: In each room, spot the one main feature that stands out.

 Rose-colored: Look past the current owner's furnishings and décor.

 Microscope: Examine all the details of the kitchen, bathrooms, and closets.

 Blindfold: Recall-What you observed and Recall-How you observed.

Repeat as necessary, making modifications based on your blindfold looking.

Instructor Teaching a Class:

 Magnifying: Spot students yawning, putting elbows on desks, or doodling.

 Binoculars: Scan the room for a different place to stand (or sit).

 Bifocals: Look to pair two students, objects, or other posted information to identify some new potential classroom dynamic to exploit.

Perform as needed. And always do blindfold looking after dismissing each class.

Art Patron Visiting an Art Museum or Gallery:

 Binoculars: Survey all the various exhibits and collections in a room at a distance.

 Magnifying: Spot one art piece to examine more closely.

 Bifocals: Look at that piece seated versus standing.

 Microscope: Scrutinize and study the details of the workmanship.

 Blindfold: Leave the area and look back at the artwork in your mind's eye.

Repeat this process in another room.

Nature Lover Taking a Walk or Hike in a Park or Other Wilderness Area:

Magnifying: Spot animal or plant life that stands out as unusual.

Bifocals: While moving, look for opposites to compare and contrast.

Binoculars: Stop and scan whenever you come upon a good vantage point.

Bifocals: While stationary, look for opposites to compare and contrast.

Move on and continue the cycle as you journey on your way.

Meeting Planner Doing a Site Inspection:

 Magnifying: Visit one room and spot one main feature.

Bifocals: Look at each room in some opposing way(s).

 Microscope: Look more closely at the entire room for additional details.

Binoculars: Step back and scan for anything you might have missed.

 Microscope: Look more closely for additional details.

Pick another room or area to visit. After exhausting every possibility:

 Blindfold: Look back and consider what was seen and not seen.

Preacher Preparing a Sermon from a Particular Text:

Magnifying: Spot words frequently used in the passage.

Bifocals: Look for various words that are easily paired as opposites.

Remember, this is not reading the text, it is just looking to see certain words before and after reading!

Now think of some other specific situations that would benefit from a looking routine. Whatever the particular circumstance, the key is to become comfortable—and skilled—in coming up with your own routines to use.

✴ 45 ✴

LOOKING EXCURSIONS

The systematic use of the Six Looking Glasses in a prearranged routine can be more formally employed in the form of a looking excursion. Sometimes called "safaris" (in search of best practices, design principles, competitive analysis, service benchmarks, experience exemplars, or a host of other objectives), these looking excursions typically involve a larger group, touring some city or venue in order to gain insights relevant to some mission for the group. For any such excursion, how the Six Looking Glasses are used will flow from the selection of destination and the purpose for seeing various sites.

Having a specific prearranged order is usually codified as a set of instructions for the group (or multiple subgroups, if a significantly larger group) to follow as the location is toured. In a sense, a looking routine is established much like those outlined in the previous chapter. The main difference is that the looking routine has been tailored to fit the place visited and the purpose of the excursion—often using a different looking routine for each tour stop.

Preparing for any such looking excursions usually involves an "advance" visit by a few individuals to the destination to scope out the options. The Six Looking Glasses can be used even in this scoping work, assisting the very process of designing the excursion—deciding where to stop and look and developing the looking routine to be used at each stop. Then the Six Looking Glasses are again used during the actual looking excursion, employing the looking routines developed from the advance scoping.

To illustrate, let's first outline how the looking glasses might be used on an advance scoping effort and then as an observation plan based on this pre-work.

ADVANCE SCOPING

Assume a team at a candy manufacturer wants to visit the Magnificent Mile in Chicago for insights on the design of a flagship store it is considering opening in its headquarters town. A few team members are sent in advance to scope the tour. This advance effort could use the Six Looking Glasses in the following ways to prepare:

 Binoculars: Before even traveling to Chicago, gather brochures, maps, and directories containing information about the various stores, restaurants, and other outlets in and around the Magnificent Mile and survey all the options. Once in Chicago, first walk the full length of Michigan Avenue, scanning all the sites at a distance, resisting the temptation to enter any specific place. Consider which side of the street to walk on and perhaps walk back on the other side. (The scanning will work best looking across the street.)

Bifocals: Consider various ways to pair opposites: one side of the street versus the other; retail stores versus restaurants; outlets on Michigan versus adjacent streets; adjacent streets parallel to Michigan versus those intersecting Michigan; outlets with direct street access versus those only accessible via multi-floor malls.

Magnifying: Throughout the advance search effort, spot places that seem most highly applicable to the candy business and/or flagship offerings.

 Microscope: Go into various places that stand out from others and examine more closely various details in these venues.

Rose-colored: Identify outlets that are most obviously or surprisingly disappointing and consider them as potential tour stops anyway.

 Blindfold: After spending time using all the other looking glasses, look back on what you may have missed or neglected.

After doing this looking to help scope the excursion, perhaps the following tour stops might be selected: American Girl Place and Disney; Apple Store and Microsoft Store (identified via bifocals); three chocolate stores—Godiva, Ghiradelli, and Hershey's (via magnifying); the showcase displays inside the "Rock and Roll" McDonald's (microscope); the slow lines at Garrett Popcorn (rose-colored); and Billy Goat Tavern (blindfold).

OBSERVATION PLAN

Let's extend this illustration further by also outlining the looking routine the advance scouts might then develop for just one of the tour stops listed previously. For example, if we consider a looking routine for visiting American Girl Place, the use of the Six Looking Glasses might flow like this:

Every place within the overall American Girl Place provides a platform for having a conversation. So have the team divide into pairs of two. Then have each team of two find some one thing they consider especially conversation-worthy by using the following looking routine:

 Binoculars: Explore every room in the place, surveying the variety of books, dolls, doll accessories, and exhibits at a distance.

Magnifying: Spot a doll to examine in greater detail.

Microscope: Scrutinize all you can about this doll, its features, its display, books about the doll's character, and its overall presentation.

 Blindfold: Go outside or into the mall hall and look back on what you observed.

Have the team gather together and dine in the restaurant, called Café. In the Café, compare and contrast the following, using

 Bifocals:

+ opposite walls,

+ ceiling and floor,

+ staff versus guests,

+ adults and children, and

+ females versus males.

Then, visit the Avenue on the way out of the Café.

Binoculars: Step back and find a vantage point. Where do you find it best for taking it all in?

 Microscope: Move left and right, away and toward the Café, from one side of the aisle to the other. What all do you see?

※

A final note: With looking excursions it is usually wise to have a handout (or field guide), recapping the observation plan with details about the looking glasses to use at each tour stop.

✳ 46 ✳

LOOKING WITH ALL FIVE SENSES

L ooking can take place with more than your eyes. True, we normally associate looking with just the eyes, because we do most all looking through our sight. But a skilled observer also looks via each of the other senses.

So look, but also listen, touch, smell, and taste. Look with all five senses. Look with your eyes, of course. But also look by listening, touching, smelling, and tasting.

Learning to look means learning to make observations. This should not be limited to just looking visually through the eye gate. Here are basic instructions for looking with all five senses:

- See the specifics.

- Listen for every sound.

- Touch what is inviting.

- Simply smell.

- Taste whatever is available (and appetizing).

These five tasks can be executed in a simple five-minute exercise. Wherever you are, take one minute per sense to look. We normally take in the world via all five senses simultaneously, but for this exercise concentrate on looking with just one sense at a time. For one minute, look with your eyes for every specific material, feature, activity, place, event, or dynamic that is present. Then shift to listening. For one minute, listen for every sound. You don't have to close your eyes to do this. Just pay attention only to what you hear. Next, for one minute, touch what is inviting. (Warning: Don't touch strangers; if you do, you might see a lawsuit!) And don't limit yourself to your hands. There are occasions when it's worthwhile to kick off your shoes and feel with your stocking (or bare) feet. Then, for one minute, smell, looking for any perfumes, deodorizers, or other aromas you might detect. Finally, for one minute, taste by eating or drinking anything that looks tasty.

Try it.

Discover how you can look with all five of your senses. You may notice that even after spending a full minute looking with your eyes, some specifics will only be noticed visually during the minute spent touching.

Let's pick a place to demonstrate using the Six Looking Glasses tool with all five senses: a waiting room in a doctor's office. A number of enterprises might benefit from looking at waiting rooms: researchers at a medical school, considering the connection between non-clinical patient experiences and medical outcomes; a pharmaceutical firm looking to add value for the physicians it serves; or, a perhaps a furniture manufacturer designing a new line for reception areas.

For our purposes here, let's look at the waiting room as if we were the office manager for a doctor's private practice. Let's now illustrate how the Six Looking Glasses might be used to look at the room using all five senses.

Binoculars: What's the best spot to see everything going on? Maybe that corner chair. What do you hear from there? How does it feel sitting in this chair, this far from the receptionist? Can you detect anything from there in the room that might give off a fragrance? Maybe that coffee station across the room. It looks like they just have coffee. Is there any other food or beverage over there to sample?

Bifocals: What two things in the room seem most opposite? What does it sound like being seated closer to the receptionist versus back in that corner? What are the hardest and softest materials here to touch? What does it smell like over by the coffee station versus away from it? Is there any juxtaposition or combination of foodstuffs or beverages to pair?

Magnifying: Look at the coffee station closely. What do you see? One single-serve coffee maker, Styrofoam cups, sugar and cream in packets, plastic (not wood) stirrers. Do you smell anything? Make a cup of coffee, so you can push the buttons. When the coffee starts brewing, notice the aroma and the sound of the machine. And when you taste the coffee, take note of all the hints of flavor.

Rose-colored: See the opportunity for improvement. Ceramic mugs with the practice's name on them, with a nice mix of colors. The cream and sugar in nicer dispensers. And a small sound system to play some soft music while the coffee brews. Maybe some high-end paper napkins, the ones that feel better than most. Also, some raw coffee beans on display to entice others with their aroma.

Microscope: Now leave this office and check out all the other doctors' offices on the floor and look at their beverage options. Check the other floors up and do a complete sensory assessment of each of their beverage options. If you like, also check out the gift shop on the first floor while you're at it.

Blindfold: Did any of the other offices stand out as really impressive? Did any of the coffee makers look or sound amazing? Were you tempted to taste a cup anywhere? Did you like the mugs in one office? If so, what about them stood out?

For each of the Six Looking Glasses we have just demonstrated how to look with all five senses, one looking glass at a time. An alternative way of organizing the looking would be to take each sense one at a time, and then cycle through each looking glass. Let's try that next.

For this demonstration, recognize that all the looking need not be completed before any thinking of taking action occurs. With Six Looking

Glasses times five senses equating to thirty looks, that's a lot of looking to perform without any thoughts or actions emerging. So, the thinking and acting derived from the looking will be noted below via these [brackets] for thoughts and these {brackets} for actions. Other commentary will be placed in these (parentheses).

Back to the doctor's office waiting room, the looking might go like this:

SIGHT

 Binoculars: What vantage point would provide the best view of everything going on? Maybe looking from the chair in the corner, or, wait, let's go farther away, out of office. Let's look online. Is there a picture of the waiting room on their website? [Let's take a picture of the waiting room, so we can post it online. Maybe we should design the space so it looks good when photographed.]

Bifocals: Notice how that one end table is cluttered with magazines, while the other table has them neatly arranged? [Should we straighten those magazines?] {Straighten cluttered magazines.} [We should have someone tidy up the magazines every half-hour.]

Magnifying: Look at this magazine. It's really old. It even has a patient's name and address label on it. [We should get a magic marker to black out the information, or just throw it away.]

Microscope: Let's examine all the magazines. How many are our own, and how many are brought in from patients? Look, three of these magazines have Bill Gates on the cover. Two have Elton John. How many different titles do we have here? And let's check all the publication dates.

 Rose-colored: What if there were only magazines with someone wearing glasses on the cover? Yes, see all the people on the covers having glasses on, since we're an ophthalmologist's office! [Regardless, we need some sort of formal magazine management.]

 Blindfold: What did you see? An online waiting room, unkempt magazines? [We could link to featured magazine articles each month on our homepage, accessible via patient smartphones. And get rid of all the germ-transmitting magazines.]

SOUND

Binoculars: Let's step outside and see if we can hear anything from the hallway. Nothing. While we're out here, we might as well walk down the hall and listen outside every office door. Again, nothing. And not only does every door sound the same, they all look the same. And the office numbers are all so small. (Note that listening triggers visual seeing. That's okay. Stressing each individual sense is not to be slavishly policed; the purpose of using all five senses is to trigger richer looking.)

Bifocals: Back inside our office, I'm going to listen to what patients say versus our receptionist. How about that? I never hear us say, "please" or "thank you." And half the patients are asking questions about the new yellow form. [We'll have to redesign that form.]

Magnifying: Okay, now let's listen to how we call patients back to the examination rooms. Hmm, every time it's last name, first name-last name. [It feels stiff, not too friendly.]

 Microscope: Now let's eavesdrop on the interaction for the next patient: How do we greet the person throughout the visit? Interesting: Only the doctor formally said, "Hello."

Rose-colored: Let's see our staff having a more courteous and friendly attitude.

 Blindfold: We need to establish a few simple verbal protocols for all of our staff. All our greetings should be friendly. [That greeting might start with some sort of artwork on the door.]

(Note that these looks could be called "binoculars listening," "bifocals listening," and so forth. But for any of the five senses it's all still looking as a skill.)

TOUCH

Rose-colored: Continuing with the idea of being friendlier, envision all staff giving each other a fist-bump when we pass each other in the hall or visit each other's desk. Not over-the-top high-fiving. Yet the little display of attitude sets an upbeat tone, and patients feel the camaraderie.

Binoculars: Let's scan all the items patients touch: door knob, clipboard, pen. They sit in a chair. They sometimes knock on the glass window when done with the forms.

Bifocals: What about standing and sitting? When standing, the feet touch the floor; when sitting, the feet still touch the floor. [What if we had a station with barstool-type chairs for filling out forms? Like a high counter against the wall at a deli.]

Magnifying: Notice the glass window. Patients sometimes tap it, but they never slide it open themselves. Only the receptionist slides the window. Check this out: The indentation on the window feels real odd to put your thumb on. It's not very inviting. [Why do we even have that glass window?]

Microscope: Let's imagine we're at the receptionist's desk and touching every item that needs to be accessed for the job. The three forms could fit in a single binder. The desktop computer could be replaced with a wireless laptop tablet to access all the records. The clipboards could be put anywhere. Maybe at a forms counter if we had one. [We could put the receptionist in the waiting room; then it could become a greeting room instead of a waiting room with a glass window barrier.]

 Blindfold: Imagine touching all the receptionist touches when not at the window.

(Note that the looking glasses need not always be used in the same sequence; here we started with rose-colored glasses for touch.)

SMELL

 Binoculars: Where do we detect any smell? Is it over by the coffee station?

 Bifocals (by the coffee station): You can't really detect much of a smell of coffee, since we're using a single-serve machine.

 Rose-colored: See only serving tea. It makes a healthier impression.

 Magnifying: Let's look through all the K-cups. Do we even have any tea options? Okay, a few chai lattes. But none of these give off much of a lingering smell either.

 Blindfold: Let's go online and research some tea-serving systems.

(Note every looking glass need not be used. Notice here that no microscope looking took place for smell.)

TASTE

 Binoculars: Where could we go besides online to see tea options? That tea store at the mall. Maybe a tea shop. [Let's see how they greet customers while we're at it!]

 Bifocals: Hot tea, iced tea. We could have both. But what other combinations could we offer in a new welcome experience? [Instead of everything being so beige, maybe a mix of deeper brown (tea) and brighter green (tea) colors would appeal to more people.]

Magnifying: What kind of candy or mints do we have in here? Do we spot any? [Let's get some tea mints.]

Microscope: I'm going to check with each staff person to find out what kind of candy or mints they have at their desk or carry. Or at least find out what everyone's favorite is. [Maybe we could have theme badges based on each staff person's favorite candy or mint. That would be a conversation starter with patients!]

 Rose-colored: For patients for whom we could obtain the information, we offer them a piece of their favorite candy or mint when they check in.

 Blindfold: This notion of favorite candy or mint could become iconic for us, in terms of striving to learn about each patient's interests.

The entire looking process flows differently depending whether you sort first by sense and then by looking glass, or alternatively, first by looking glass and then by sense. Try both ways.

The Six Looking Glasses method need not be used in conjunction with using each and every sense. The purpose of combining a sensory assessment with the Six Looking Glasses here is to make clear that looking need not be done only with your eyes.

To conclude, let me share a few sense-specific points.

Regarding touch: Consider touching with your feet in this particular manner: Walk! Walking is a richly practical means of looking. Each of the Six Looking Glasses can be used while walking.

Regarding smell: Feel free to "smell a rat." Look for things that simply don't make sense or seem contradictory. If nothing more, this is a great means to set up bifocals looking or rose-colored-glasses looking.

Regarding taste: Ask yourself, "What sense of taste is evoked?" In many situations, this form of rose-colored-glasses looking is essential, particularly when there is no food or beverage available. Similarly, you could ask, "What sense of smell is evoked?" in the absence of any aromas. The question is only really needed for taste and smell, as there is most always something to see, hear, or touch.

Again, the main reason for addressing all five senses is to encourage looking with more than just your eyes. Look for occasions to use all Six Looking Glasses one sense at a time.

☀ 47 ☀

CAPTURING WHAT YOU SEE

B lindfold looking used the simple two categories of gems and gaps to look back with that one looking glass at what has been seen. Now we will introduce a more systematic checklist for capturing what has been seen with any or all of the Six Looking Glasses collectively—whether used during everyday looking, via a formal routine, or while on an excursion.

Consider these ten categories a post-looking as well as a pre-thinking framework. Like the optic nerve, the checklist connects the eye to the brain. Use the checklist as a series of prompts to evaluate and capture what has been seen, turning looking efforts into looking outcomes.

Observations: the most basic assessment of looking outcomes

- What did you observe?
- Simply: What did you see?

Particulars: observations of a more specific kind, identifying nuances

- What was particularly evident?
- Pointedly: What specific observations did you make?

Technicalities: even more specific observations or particulars
about the particulars

• What technical dimensions did you observe?

• Functionally: What did you see about how something worked?

Information: observations of openly revealed diagrams,
pictures, text, or even data

• What information was on display?

• Openly: What did you see intentionally exhibited?

Concerns: observations that identified difficulties, problems, or
other concerns

• What did you see that raises some concern?

• Cautiously: What did you see that could pose some
potential issue?

Notables: observations that stood out as especially noteworthy

• What did you see as "signature" elements or moments?

• Significantly: What did you see as highlights or high points?

Edges: observations at the end of one thing and beginning
of another

• What boundaries and borders were apparent?

• Decidedly: What did you see betwixt and between various sights?

Revelations: observations of a totally unexpected nature

- What did you see that was completely foreign to prior experience?
- Surprisingly: What did you see that you never before saw?

Value Opportunities: observations that pointed to ways to generate value

- What opportunities to add value did you see?
- Practically: What did you see that suggested new means of creating value?

Extraneous Items: seemingly insignificant matters that were nevertheless noticed

- What else did you see that has not been captured?
- Additionally: What else did you see?

Ask yourself: What were your observations? What particulars were noticed? What technicalities were seen at work? What information was displayed? What concerns were evident? Also, what else was notable? What edges between various sights were detected? What revelations were revealed? What value opportunities were seen? Were any extraneous items seen?

Use the checklist to thoroughly and richly capture the observations you make using the Six Looking Glasses. Your time and effort spent looking will ultimately yield benefits only if you stop looking and list your observations and insights.

LOOK HERE

As we have made our way through this book, the explanation of the Six Looking Glasses tool has largely aimed to serve as fodder for subsequent thinking. For indeed, observational insights can and should trigger practical new ideas that can be acted upon. Recall this simple progression from the Introduction:

Looking ⟼ *Thinking* ⟼ *Acting*

We have already examined one alternative target for looking, introduced via one of the Six Looking Glasses, namely blindfold looking. Blindfold looking looks at looking; that's its aim here:

Looking ⟼ *Thinking* ⟼ *Acting*
↑
Looking

In addition, the last chapter outlined a ten-point checklist that aims looking at the process of converting looks into thoughts, as shown here:

Looking ⟼ *Thinking* ⟼ *Acting*
⬆

Observations
Particulars
Technicalities
Information
Concerns
Notables
Edges
Revelations
Value Opportunities
Extraneous items

Let's add three more directions in which looking can be aimed.

First, looking can be aimed at the inner mechanics of thinking. Let's be clear: This is not thinking about thinking. (That would involve Dr. de Bono's Blue Hat thinking from his Six Hat method.) Rather, it's just looking at how thinking is outwardly practiced. Looking at thinking examines whether the thinking was performed individually or as a group, silently or verbally (some people think by talking), formally structured (with tools like Six Hats) or in free-form. You can aim looking at the mechanics of thinking:

Looking ⟼ *Thinking* ⟼ *Acting*
⬆

Solo or group?
Silent or verbal?
Structured or free-form?

Also, you can observe the process of converting thoughts into actions. It's usually a mistake to jump immediately from thought to action. Often new ideas need to be tested or tried on an experimental basis, prototyped, validated via controlled studies, or carefully launched. So looking with looking glasses can be directed here:

Looking ⟶ *Thinking* ⟶ *Acting*

↑

Tests/Trials

Prototypes

Validations

Launches

Finally, looking can look at any primary activity and try to detect various attitudes, behaviors, and motivations behind, beneath, and under the action:

Looking ⟶ *Thinking* ⟶ *Acting*

↑

Attitudes

Behaviors

Motivations

Finally—armed with the Six Looking Glasses—it's time to go look!

APPENDICES

A

LOOK AT YOURSELF:
A SELF-ASSESSMENT

I n chapter 2, it was pointed out that "how you see yourself influences what you see when you look." Let's extend that thought, adding that how you see yourself may also influence what looking glasses you might be predisposed to use most often; or more significantly, might be predisposed to neglect to use as often as you should, or even ignore altogether.

Following is a simple self-assessment.

Listed are six statements. Read them all, and then force-rank the statements in the order in which you believe they describe yourself. Get out a pen or pencil and fill in the blanks (1-2-3-4-5-6). Be honest with yourself, but don't over-analyze. Just number the statements in the order that best represents how you see yourself.

_____ *"I'm not a detail person."*

_____ *"I'm always interested in finding the next big thing."*

_____ *"I cannot stand making mistakes."*

_____ *"I like to find the one best way to do anything."*

_____ *"I am easily distracted."*

_____ *"I'm a stickler for details."*

How do you see yourself? Depending on how you see yourself, you may need to make an extra effort to use certain looking glasses. It may behoove you to practice using looking glasses that you might be predisposed to neglect. At least be aware of your preferences.

Consider your #1 ranked statement:

If you ranked as first, "I'm a stickler for details," then you may need to make an extra effort to use binoculars looking. Practice surveying and scanning. It will help you prioritize some details over others.

If you ranked as first, "I like to find the one best way to do anything," then you may benefit from greater use of bifocals. Practice comparing and contrasting. It may help you see alternatives that are better yet.

If you ranked as first, "I am easily distracted," then you may need to make an extra effort to do magnifying-glass looking. Practice pausing and pinpointing. It may help you be less distracted and actually help you develop new interests.

If you ranked as first, "I'm not a detail person," then you may need to make an extra effort to use microscope looking. Practice scrutinizing and studying. It will force you to better appreciate what there is to see in the weeds.

If you ranked as first, "I cannot stand to make mistakes," then you may benefit from greater use of rose-colored glasses. Practice enhancing and enriching what you see. It may help you uncover more opportunities to perfect.

If you ranked as first, "I'm always interested in finding the next big thing," you may need to make an extra effort to use blindfolds. Practice more looking at looking. It may make you realize the next big thing might be found in a previous little thing.

Your #2 and #3 ranked statements might be similarly assessed. You might find you need to make an extra effort to use more than one looking glass or to make a point of practicing more than one.

Over time, you may want to circle back and reassess your self-assessment ranking. You might find that with actual use of the Six Looking Glasses tool—and the more you see from making more and better observations— that your view of yourself changes.

✳ **B** ✳

CONSTRUCTION OF THE
SIX LOOKING GLASSES

Especially for those readers familiar with Dr. de Bono's Six Thinking Hats and Six Action Shoes methods, this appendix offers some added background on the construction of the Six Looking Glasses vis-à-vis those other frameworks. Other readers may also find this perspective of additional benefit as well.

Theoretically, the looking glasses could be depicted by assigning each a specific color. This could certainly be done to make them more visually appealing in print. But frankly, there would be no other practical reason to refer to any of the looking glasses by color (other than rose-colored glasses, the color of which is always downplayed).

This is a departure from the use of color in Dr. de Bono's Six Thinking Hats and Six Action Shoes methods. Let me explain.

For the Six Thinking Hats, color is essential to understanding the functionality of each hat. Each thinking mode is just a "hat," not a different type of hat (e.g., top hat, baseball cap, beret, etc.); color alone signals the different mode of thinking: Red Hat (feelings and emotion, like "red hot"); White Hat (neutral facts, like paper); Yellow Hat (logical positive; like sunshine); Black Hat (logical negative, like a judge's robe); Green Hat (creativity, growing ideas like grass); Blue Hat (thinking about thinking, like the sky overhead). The colors help recall the function of each hat. In fact, the six thinking modes/hats are known exclusively by their respective color, and this suffices in easily recalling which hat is which.

For the Six Action Shoes, color is also part of the description of each style of action. The colors help convey each function—navy (drills and routines, like in the Navy), grey (investigating, as through a fog), brown (gritty work, like the dirty ground), orange (emergency steps, like safety cones), pink (compassionate caring, a softer color), purple (authoritative steps, an imperial color). But the shoes are also different types, further aiding in the recall of what kind of action each represents—formal shoes (formal procedures), sneakers (sneaky exploration), brogues (practical behavior), gumboots (rescue work), slippers (adding comfort), and riding boots (riding high above others). The Six Action Shoes are known via the combination of color and type: Navy Formal Shoes, Grey Sneakers, Brown Brogues, Orange Gumboots, Pink Slippers, and Purple Riding Boots.

For the Six Thinking Hats and Six Action Shoes methods, the use of color or color-and-type is a necessarily contrived mechanism to distinguish each hat or each shoe, and to help remember each function. For the Six Hats method, color suffices to do this job; for the Six Shoes method, both color and type are evidently helpful.

In constructing the Six Looking Glasses tool, this had to be addressed: What would best serve as the means to clearly distinguish and recall each lens?

Three options presented themselves:

1. use of color alone,

2. use of color and type, or alternatively,

3. use of type alone.

Color alone is obviously not the desired approach, given the names of glasses already refer to types. To also refer to each looking glass by color would be adding color just for the sake of adding color.

So referring to the type of looking glass alone suffices to understand each way of looking. (The logic here is similar to that for Six Hats method: Referring to each hat by some type would be adding a type of hat just for the sake of adding type, when color alone suffices to understand each mode of thinking.)

I hope you'll agree that the resulting Six Looking Glasses (sans reliance on referencing color) together offer a more-than-adequate set of viewfinders with which to make a rich mix of observations.

ACKNOWLEDGMENTS

My thanks go to Greg Bogue, Cameron Carter, Kyle Coolbroth, Mark Greiner, Doug Parker, and Grady Powell for reading early manuscripts of this book and offering valuable feedback. I would also like to thank Bob Fee for encouraging me to experiment with the Six Looking Glasses in class at SCAD while the tool was in its infancy, Lee Knight and Dee Silfies for letting me develop a more polished version of the technique in educational sessions at ExhibitorLive, and David Zahl and Ethan Richardson for allowing me to share the framework in the context of "looking in an age of distraction" at Mockingbird's annual conference.

Thanks also to Justin Branch, Rachael Brandenburg, Diana Ceres, Steve Elizalde, Jen Glynn, Chelsea Richards, Abbey Sieger, Nathan True, and the crew at Greenleaf Book Group for donning rose-colored glasses and seeing the potential in this project and helping turn it into a published reality. And thanks to Davis Szalay for the design of the six icons used for the looking glasses.

I am indebted to my business partners at Strategic Horizons LLP, Joe Pine and Doug Parker, for their constant support, including their encouragement to pursue this tome. Thanks, partners!

Two people merit special thanks: Sally Harrison-Pepper for calling me a "professional observer" some ten plus years ago—leading me to see myself differently; and Paul Miller for pointing out the significant role that looking played in the loving life of Jesus—leading me to better appreciate the personal need to see others more intently.

Thanks are due to my wife Beth and children Evan and Anna, for putting up with my many looking lapses at home. Thanks for loving me nonetheless.

Finally, I must express dear thanks to my parents, Haydn and E. Jean Gilmore, for repeatedly reading *Stop Look Listen* to me as a child and for urging me to be ever looking out the backseat windows of our 1959 and 1969 Chevy Impalas. It was there where I first loved to look.

ABOUT THE AUTHOR

Jim Gilmore coauthored the highly influential book, *The Experience Economy: Work Is Theatre & Every Business a Stage* (Harvard Business School Press). Now published in eighteen languages—and in an updated paperback edition—the book spawned worldwide interest in experience design, experiential marketing, and customer experience management.

Jim's other book, *Authenticity: What Consumers Really Want* (Harvard Business Review Press), prompted *TIME* magazine in a March 2008 cover story to name its insight on the subject as one of "Ten ideas that are changing the world."

Jim is co-founder of Strategic Horizons LLP, based in Aurora, Ohio. He is a Batten Fellow and adjunct lecturer at the Darden Graduate School of Business at the University of Virginia, where he teaches a course on the Experience Economy. Gilmore is also a visiting lecturer in Apologetics at Westminster Seminary California, where he teaches a course on cultural hermeneutics. He also teaches a design course at the Weatherhead School of Management at Case Western Reserve University.

He is a graduate of the Wharton School of the University of Pennsylvania, an alumnus of Procter & Gamble, and before co-founding Strategic Horizons LLP was head of CSC Consulting's Process Innovation practice.

Jim can be reached at jim@strategichorizons.com.